Origins of the Maritime Strategy

MICHAEL A. PALMER

Origins of the Maritime Strategy

The Development of American Naval Strategy,
1945–1955

Sponsored by the Naval Historical Center

NAVAL INSTITUTE PRESS
Annapolis, Maryland

Originally published as *Origins of the Maritime Strategy: American Naval Strategy in the First Postwar Decade* in 1988 by the Naval Historical Center.

Photographs identified by the prefix NH are Naval Historical Center photographs. All others are held in Still Pictures Branch, National Archives, Washington, D.C. 20408.

Printed in the United States of America on acid-free paper ∞

9 8 7 6 5 4 3 2
First Printing

Library of Congress Cataloging-in-Publication Data

Palmer, Michael A.
    Origins of the maritime strategy : the development of American naval strategy, 1945–1955 / Michael A. Palmer.
        p.   cm.
    Includes bibliographical references.
    ISBN 0-87021-667-8
    1. Sea-power—United States—History—20th century.   2. Naval strategy.   3. United States. Navy—History—20th century.   I. Title.
VA59.P283   1990
359'.03'0973—dc20   —dc20   90-30117
                                                                    CIP

Contents

Illustrations

Foreword

THE 1980s were exciting times to be in the United States Navy. At sea, the Navy successfully engaged in a wide range of operations carrying out American foreign and defense policies and an equally wide range of exercises introducing new systems and tactical concepts into the fleet. Ashore, the Navy experienced money-saving managerial and procurement reforms, strong domestic public and political support, and a renaissance in strategic thinking.

This last development was tightly interwoven with all the others. Among its best-known manifestations were the promulgation of the Maritime Strategy in Washington; an outpouring of thoughtful related writings by naval officers and interested civilians; and reinvigorated research, teaching, and war-gaming activities at the Naval War College in Newport.

The Navy's intellectual renaissance was also characterized by a revitalization of the programs of the Naval Historical Center, including the creation of a new Contemporary History Branch. Not surprisingly, in view of the mutually supporting and interrelated nature of the Navy's across-the-board revival, one of that branch's first and most stimulating products was Dr. Michael Palmer's 1988 *Origins of the Maritime Strategy.*

An instant sensation and immediate "must" reading for American naval officers and civilian naval specialists, *Origins* has fortunately now been made available to a much wider reading public through the good offices of the U.S. Naval Institute (yet another institution that contributed enormously to the great American naval reawakening of the 1980s).

In *Origins,* Dr. Palmer set out deliberately to teach those of us who shared in that reawakening a number of lessons, and he succeeded admirably. These lessons are clearly laid out in the book, and most would gain little from any extensive discussion here. Three, however, seem to me to merit some small degree of foreshadowing and emphasis:

First, the nation derives extraordinary benefits from the combat power, mobility, and flexibility of its Navy.

Second, the Navy derives equally extraordinary benefits from a clear, up-to-date, open formulation of its underlying strategy (with the inevitable—and desirable—concomitant public debate).

Third, strategy formulation derives equally extraordinary benefits from well-argued writing efforts in contemporary naval history, both inside and outside of government.

Our challenge now—readers and writers, users and thinkers, operators and strategists together—is to ensure that the nation of the 1990s and the twenty-first century, and its Navy and strategic thinking, will gain as much from the books yet to come as those of the 1980s have gained from *Origins of the Maritime Strategy.*

Peter M. Swartz
Captain, United States Navy

Acknowledgments

I must acknowledge the help of Captain Peter M. Swartz, USN, in initiating, stimulating, and focusing this study which originated in a discussion that followed his fall 1986 briefing on the Maritime Strategy. Captain Swartz recommended that I address the similarities between the Navy's current and postwar strategies in an article. That projected piece soon became the proposal for a short history. Again, Captain Swartz, a member of the Secretary of the Navy's Advisory Committee on Naval History, supported the idea. Throughout the writing of this work he has remained an invaluable supporter, source of information, advisor, and friend. He critiqued several drafts of the manuscript. His useful annotated bibliographies (cited among the sources for this study) are far more than lists of secondary works relevant to the study of the Maritime Strategy of the 1980s, for they offer sources and comments on the whole of the U.S. Navy's postwar strategy. They represent the fruits not only of Captain Swartz's first-hand experience as a professional officer involved in formulating the Maritime Strategy but also his personal research as a scholar of the postwar Navy.

I must offer my appreciation to Admirals Robert B. Carney and Arleigh A. Burke and Rear Admirals Herbert H. Anderson, Ira H. Nunn, and J. C. Wylie for granting me interviews and, in the case of Admiral Burke, access to his oral history.

Dr. Ronald H. Spector, Director of Naval History, supported the project and reviewed the manuscript, as did the Center's Senior Historian, Dr. Dean C. Allard, for which I am especially grateful.

Dr. Edward J. Marolda, head of the Naval Historical Center's Contemporary History Branch, was quick to support my proposal for a short history. My work benefitted tremendously from his editorial skills and knowledge of the period.

Dr. Malcolm Muir, the Center's Visiting Scholar; Captain Roger W. Barnett, USN (Ret.), no stranger to the Maritime Strategy; and Dr. Thomas Hone, who sat through many a lunchtime discussion as he worked on his own short history, also reviewed the manuscript.

Within the Contemporary History Branch, Ms. Sandra Doyle edited the final draft of the manuscript and prepared the index. Her professional skills are much appreciated. Drs. Theresa Kraus, Clarence Wunderlin, and Jeffrey Barlow graciously commented on the manuscript.

Mr. Charles Haberlein, head of the Photographic Section, not only helped select illustrations for the work but also reviewed the manuscript and offered many worthwhile suggestions.

The friendly archivists from the Operational Archives Branch, especially Mr. Wes Pryce, Mr. Bernard Cavalcante, Ms. Judy Short, and Ms. Kathy Rohr, were always helpful.

The staff of the Navy Department Library provided invaluable assistance as usual, especially Mr. John Vajda and Ms. Sandy Kay.

And I must also thank my wife, Carol. As always, my work found its way home, and my spouse once again was forced to learn about yet another facet of naval history.

All errors of fact and interpretation are my own.

Abbreviations

ABC	American, British, and Canadian
ACNO	Assistant Chief of Naval Operations
ASW	Antisubmarine Warfare
BNEP	Basic Naval Establishment Plan
CCS	Combined Chiefs of Staff
CINCNELM	Commander in Chief U.S. Naval Forces, Eastern Atlantic and Mediterranean (former COMNAVEASTLANTMED)
CINCPAC	Commander in Chief, Pacific
CINCPACFLT	Commander in Chief, U.S. Pacific Fleet
COMINCH	Commander in Chief, U.S. Fleet
COMNAVMED	Commander U.S. Naval Forces, Mediterranean
COMNAVNAW	Commander U.S. Naval Forces, Northwest African Waters
CNO	Chief of Naval Operations
COMSUBPAC	Commander Submarines, Pacific
COMSUBLANT	Commander Submarines, Atlantic
COS	Chief of Staff
CVA	Attack Aircraft Carrier
CVB	*Midway*-class Aircraft Carrier
DCNO	Deputy Chief of Naval Operations
DOD	Department of Defense

G-I-UK	Greenland-Iceland-United Kingdom
JANAID	Joint Army-Navy Air Intelligence Division
JCS	Joint Chiefs of Staff
JPS	Joint Staff Planners
NAORPG	North Atlantic Ocean Regional Planning Group
NSC	National Security Council
NSPS	Naval Strategic Planning Study
OEG	Operations Evaluation Group
ONI	Office of Naval Intelligence
OPNAV	Office of the Chief of Naval Operations
PHPC	Post-Hostilities Planning Committee
SACLANT	Supreme Allied Commander, Atlantic
SCOROR	Secretary's Committee on Research on Reorganization
SHAEF	Supreme Headquarters Allied Expeditionary Force
SLOC	Sea Lines of Communication
SOSUS	Sound Surveillance System
SSBN	Nuclear-powered Ballistic Missile Submarine
SWNCC	State-War-Navy Coordinating Committee
UNICOM	Unification Committee
USNI	United States Naval Institute
VCNO	Vice Chief of Naval Operations

Origins of the Maritime Strategy

Introduction

THE Maritime Strategy is often portrayed as something new, a radical strategic departure on the part of the United States Navy, a creation of the Reagan administration, and a rationale for Secretary of the Navy John Lehman's 600-ship Navy.[1] But, as Chief of Naval Operations (CNO) Admiral Carlisle A. H. Trost wrote, the Maritime Strategy "was not—and is not—a force builder, and it was certainly not the origin of the 600-ship Navy."[2] The Maritime Strategy predates the election of 1980 and Lehman's appointment as Secretary of the Navy.

The immediate origin of the Maritime Strategy can be traced to the Pacific in 1977 where Admiral Thomas B. Hayward, Commander in Chief, U.S. Pacific Fleet (CINCPACFLT), developed Sea Strike, a plan that envisioned a carrier task group offensive against Soviet Far Eastern bases in the event of war.[3]

As CNO two years later, Hayward outlined in testimony before Congress his strategic approach, listing several principles that formed the core of what is now termed the "Maritime Strategy."[4] Hayward believed that a NATO-Warsaw Pact conflict would "inevitably be worldwide in scope." To meet that challenge, the Navy would have to be "offensively capable." He told Congress: "The geographic range of the Navy's responsibilities is too broad, and its forces far too small, to adopt a defensive, reactive posture in a worldwide conflict with the Soviet Union." The U.S. Navy would have to carry "the war to the enemy's naval forces with the objective of achieving the earliest possible destruction of his capability to interfere with our use of the sea areas essential for support of our own forces and allies." To

Hayward, carrier battle groups, representing the American technological lead over the Soviets, were "optimally suited for the execution of this strategy." That edge would have to be maintained. The
Navy would also have to

> exploit Soviet geographic disadvantages and continue to deploy
> naval forces in locales which provide us strategic advantage. It is
> important that we make the Soviets understand that in war there
> will be no sanctuaries for their forces. Keeping the Soviets pre-
> occupied with defensive concerns locks up Soviet naval forces in
> areas close to the USSR, limiting their availability for campaigns
> against the SLOCs [sea lines of communication], or for operations
> in support of offensive thrusts on the flanks of NATO or elsewhere,
> such as in the Middle East or in Asia.

Hayward called for the integration of the American naval effort
with that of the other services and the nation's allies. The U.S. Navy's
"current narrow margin" of advantage left no alternative. Hayward
stressed the importance of skillful operational performance by commanders, who in executing this strategy would have to be bound by
the "concept of calculated risk," and who, it was hoped, would win
for the United States future victories.

Hayward's call was not so much for a larger service, as it was for a
revitalization of the Navy. He spoke not of 600 ships, nor of fifteen-
carrier battle groups. He accepted the Carter Defense Department's
minimum of twelve, although he admitted that his force posture desires were "substantially higher." The physical and psychological decline of a post-Vietnam Navy faced with increasing global demands
and an expanding Soviet Navy made such a reinvigoration essential.
Lacking quantity, the Navy would need quality—good leaders, sailors, material, and a coherent strategic concept.[5]

The Maritime Strategy debate that began midway through the
presidency of Jimmy Carter should be seen within the context of the
contemporary national renaissance of military thought. This recon-
sideration of nuclear and conventional strategy, operations, and tactics continues. Interest in reform, initiative, operational art, and maneuver exhibits a healthy rebirth of thinking in the national defense
establishment.

The United States Army, probably the service most shaken by the
Vietnam experience, was the first to embark on a search for a new

doctrine. The post-Vietnam Army officially embraced defensive doctrine in the 1976 version of its operational manual, FM 100-5, which in the words of one critic, "elevated [Dunkirk] to the status of a force design concept."[6] But Active Defense prompted a debate within and without the Army. The doctrine was criticized for its "disregard of the tactical imponderables like initiative, morale, and the offensive spirit; for its apparent exaltation of firepower over maneuver; and for its preoccupation with calculations of relative attrition to the exclusion of tactical creativity and judgement."[7]

The debate of the late 1970s and early 1980s resulted in the issuance of a new edition of FM 100-5 embodying the "AirLand Battle concept" during the same year, 1982, that the Navy promulgated the Maritime Strategy. AirLand Battle called for "securing or retaining the initiative and exercising it aggressively to defeat the enemy. Destruction of the opposing force is achieved by throwing the enemy off balance with powerful initial blows from unexpected directions and then following up rapidly to prevent recovery."[8]

The Maritime Strategy and the AirLand Battle were reactions to the following: the over accentuation on operational analysis that reduced war to a numerical exercise, best tested in computer simulations in which humans were removed from the "loop"; the defensive missions given the services in the event of war; the national strategy of forward defense in support of allies facing quantitatively superior aggressor forces; and the post-Vietnam retrenchment mentality.

Colonel Richard Hart Sinnreich observed: the "opening lines from FM 100-5's [1982] chapter on 'Combat Fundamentals' would have surprised neither Patton nor MacArthur—nor even, for that matter, Hannibal or Frederick the Great." They represented "a return to basics."[9] So it was with Hayward's call for an offensive strategy, one that rejected direct defense of the SLOCs as its primary mission. Hayward's ideas, too, wrote Captain Peter M. Swartz, represented a renaissance not a birth, "a return to concepts familiar to U.S. naval officers of the first post-World War II decade."[10]

It was in that decade that the U.S. Navy came face to face with geopolitical reality. The Soviets controlled the heartland of Eurasia and seemed a dominant, nearly hegemonic land power. Samuel P. Huntington termed the dilemma that of a "transoceanic navy" facing the question, "How could the Navy play a role in applying American power to the European continent?" Huntington outlined in 1954

what would come to be called the Maritime Strategy. He rejected
SLOC protection as a principal mission and focused instead on the
offensive:

> [Antisubmarine warfare] can never become the primary mission of
> the Navy. For it is a defensive operation designed to protect the
> Navy's base, *i.e.,* its control and utilization of the sea, and this base
> is maintained so that the Navy can perform its important offensive
> operations against shore targets. . . . It is a secondary mission, the
> effective performance of which, however, is essential to the perfor-
> mance of its primary mission. And, indeed, the successful accom-
> plishment of the primary mission of the Navy—the maintenance
> of American power along the littoral—will in itself be the most
> important factor in protecting the Navy's base. For holding the lit-
> toral will drastically limit the avenues of access of Soviet sub-
> marines to the high seas.[11]

At the same time, Huntington considered three related elements
essential in shaping the purpose or role of a service in implementing
national policy. The first, and most important, he termed the *"strategic concept . . .* how, when, and where the military service expects to
protect the nation against some threat to its security." In the absence
of such a concept, the service "wallows about amid a variety of con-
flicting and confusing goals, and ultimately it suffers both physical
and moral degeneration." Second, a service must gain *"public support,"* the acquisition and maintenance of which is easier if a clearly
stated strategic concept exists. Huntington stressed that the service
itself had "the responsibility to develop this necessary support."
Third, the service must develop an *"organizational structure"* tailored
to support the strategic concept. The more clearly the latter is defined, the simpler the task. This structure, throughout all levels, must
meet the requirements of the service, which may differ from other
services and may also change over time.[12]

Huntington rejected what many insisted should be the Navy's
primary mission, for example, John J. Mearsheimer's assertion: "the
Navy can counter [the Soviet submarine] threat with a defensive sea
control strategy. It is not necessary or desirable to adopt an offensive
strategy to protect the SLOCs. . . . NATO does not need an offensive
sea control strategy. In fact, NATO's deterrent posture would be
better served by the defensive alternative."[13]

Huntington's emphasis on an offensive strategic concept that strengthens the nation's security, gains public support, and shapes the service's organization is reflected in Admiral James D. Watkins's comments on the Maritime Strategy.

> [It] offers a global perspective to operational commanders and provides a foundation for advice to the National Command Authorities. The strategy has become the key element in shaping Navy programmatic decisions. It is of equal value as a vehicle for shaping and disseminating a professional consensus on warfighting where it matters—at sea.[14]

Captain Linton F. Brooks, another proponent of the Maritime Strategy, frankly admitted that it "has unquestionably contributed to the Navy's success in articulating and justifying programs before Congress."[15]

◆ ◆ ◆

The primary intent of this study is to outline the development of the Navy's postwar strategic concept. Of secondary importance, given time and space constraints, are points of comparison and contrast with the Maritime Strategy of the 1980s and the reasons for the "loss" of the Navy's initial postwar strategic concept in the mid-1950s.

As Admiral Trost wrote, the questions the Navy sought to answer in the early 1980s with the Maritime Strategy were not new: "Over the years our Maritime Strategy has been very much like the British Constitution—unwritten but thoroughly understood by those who must practice it." That was indeed true for Trost's early career, for he entered active service in 1953 just as the Navy's postwar strategic concept began to erode, just as Huntington made his plea for a "transoceanic navy" in the pages of the U.S. Naval Institute *Proceedings*.[16]

That Huntington felt compelled to address the issue in 1954 indicates that nearly a decade after the end of the Second World War the Navy had failed to annunciate publicly that which he considered fundamental—a clearly stated, offensive, strategic concept for applying power against a nonnaval, nonmaritime state. In his study of defense policy published in 1962, Vincent Davis noted the same shortcoming. For a Navy reared on the works of Alfred Thayer Mahan and blooded in Pacific battles, the transition from an "oceanic" to a "transoceanic" outlook was difficult. Nevertheless, the U.S. Navy made a remarkably rapid, effective transition once the nation's political leaders gave the necessary direction. While it is true that the post-war era produced no Mahan, able officers, most notably Vice Admiral Forrest P. Sherman, formulated in 1946 and 1947 the strategic concept so necessary to the service—a clearly defined maritime strategy, one rediscovered and resurrected four decades later. The Navy possessed a written strategy in the immediate postwar period, one that resembles to a great extent the Maritime Strategy of the 1980s. Ironically, the strategic concept outlined by Huntington in 1954 was not one in need of discovery, but one in the process of being lost.

1 · *The Challenge of Victory*

In the summer of 1945, historian Stefan T. Possony reviewed the course of the world's most destructive war and recognized in it the "Vindication of Sea Power."[1] The submarine menace had been mastered in the Atlantic. Air power, far from supplanting naval power, had been integrated with it and applied with deadly effectiveness. Those who in the decades between the world wars had doubted the viability of navies had been proven wrong.

The outcome of the Second World War vindicated the U.S. Navy, overshadowed for more than a century and a half by a larger, more experienced, tradition-rich Royal Navy. The American service followed British examples. Alfred Thayer Mahan turned to the naval history of Great Britain to illustrate his principles of sea power. The U.S. Navy of 1941 had yet to win its Trafalgar, had yet to test itself in battle against a first-class enemy in a fleet action. But in the course of the 1941–45 war, the American Navy achieved unquestioned pre-eminence at sea, not only in quantity but also in quality. Its Pacific victories, too numerous to list, marked the coming of age of the American service. A battle-hardened force now stood ready to accept the mantle so long borne by the Royal Navy. The U.S. Navy at last had attained its destiny.

But if the war had vindicated American sea power, had victory made it irrelevant? Possony wrote of what navies had accomplished, not what navies might do in the future. His article appeared in the September issue of the U.S. Naval Institute *Proceedings* as the atomic age dawned. Civilian strategist Bernard Brodie wrote in the January 1946 issue of *Foreign Affairs:* "the Navy's indubitably superb accomplishment in the greatest of all naval wars will not facilitate its taking the lead in revaluing its own place in the national security."[2]

The very scope of the American naval victory planted the seeds of the Navy's demise. At the end of any successful war there would, of course, be reductions in force—demobilization. But additional perils confronted the Navy in 1945. The atomic bomb reopened the interwar debate on the vulnerability and use of naval forces. Many "Mitchellites" saw in the nuclear destruction of Hiroshima and Nagasaki the end of navies, and perhaps all but strategic air forces.[3] Unification of the American armed forces threatened to reduce the Navy's overall size and function in national defense.[4] Critics wondered what role the U.S. Navy would play now that its major antagonist—Japan—was reduced to ruins, its fleet destroyed.

Even before the end of the Second World War, naval leaders planned for the postwar period. Both the military and civilians in the naval establishment agreed that the United States should maintain a sizeable fleet at war's end. The Navy, not surprisingly, took the lesson of Pearl Harbor most seriously. Postwar naval strength was a common theme of wartime speeches and articles. In a September 1942 address at his alma mater, Princeton University, then Undersecretary of the Navy James V. Forrestal insisted "that never again shall the nation be permitted to discard its arms and to rely upon the protocols of good faith and general statements of good-will."[5]

Prewar thought shaped the Navy's plans for the postwar world. The works of Mahan and his interpreters dominated the thinking of many American naval officers. With its focus on the Pacific, the interwar Navy prepared for a struggle with the Imperial Japanese Navy that would ultimately involve operations in the far reaches of the Western Pacific and climax in a decisive battle. American naval officers believed their destiny lay in the Pacific where they would fight and win their Trafalgar. The Atlantic theater held no comparable attraction. After the surrender of the German High Seas Fleet at the end of the Great War, a German threat became remote. Great Britain posed an unlikely enemy. In a future global war American naval officers would safeguard the security of the Western Hemisphere by assuming the strategic defensive in the Western Atlantic.[6]

Such thinking was entirely appropriate for the period characterized by Huntington as the "oceanic" phase of American history that began with the American naval buildup at the close of the nineteenth century.[7] During the preceding "continental" phase, from 1775 to the 1890s, "those threats which arose to the national security were generally dealt with on land, and sea power consequently played a subordinate role in the implementation of national policy." The projection of American interests and power across the seas in the "oceanic" phase, the acquisition of overseas territories, and involvement in the European and Asian power balances led the United States to seek "supremacy" on the oceans, just as it had on the North American continent. Mahan provided the strategic concept: command of the seas with concentrated battle fleets designed to destroy those of the enemy in a decisive engagement. Most naval officers, congressmen, and the public readily comprehended such a concept, ensuring political and popular support for the Navy to remain the senior service, the nation's "first line of defense."

The "oceanic" phase ended abruptly in 1945. No nation remained to challenge American naval power. The new era demanded a new way of thinking, a new strategic concept. As Huntington wrote: "A military service capable of meeting one threat to the national security loses its reason for existence when that threat weakens or disappears. If the service is to continue to exist, it must develop a new strategic concept related to some other security threat."[8] For the U.S. Navy that meant a shift in focus: from the Pacific to the Atlantic, and from the oceans to the surrounding shores.

The Navy gradually recognized that the American goal in the "transoceanic" phase was not only to retain command of the sea but also to project power ashore, "more specifically . . . to that decisive strip of littoral encircling the Eurasian continent." Despite the "Europe First" grand strategy pursued during the war and the elimination of the Imperial Japanese Navy as a rival, the Navy's Pacific focus and prewar outlook persisted.[9] Secretary of the Navy Frank Knox, speaking in Chicago in December 1943, described a postwar "working agreement between the British and American navies which assigns to the British fleets control of the Eastern Atlantic, the Mediterranean and the Indian Ocean. The U.S. Navy guards the Western Atlantic and the entire Pacific. . . . There is the backbone of the postwar naval police force, already organized and functioning."[10] Knox's successor, Forrestal, wrote in the July 1945 issue of *Sea Power:* "Both our own national security and our contribution to international stability will require naval forces, including bases, which will assure control of the Western Atlantic Ocean and the Pacific Ocean."[11] Knox's and Forrestal's visions of the Navy's role in the postwar world reflected both prewar thought and the service's early plans.[12]

Navy wartime planners faced serious difficulties shaping a coherent program for an uncertain postwar world, for neither Congress nor the administration offered substantial guidance. Only gradually did the "doctrine of national security" develop into a framework for policy makers.[13] To Navy planners, strong pressure from the American people to reduce the size of the armed forces and the budgets that supported them was certain. The demilitarization of the Axis powers and the operation of the Grand Alliance within the framework of an international organization were fundamental precepts of American national policy.[14] Both potential threats to American security and the extent of public and congressional support for a sizeable Navy were unclear. Moreover, it became evident towards the end of the war that the Navy faced not only the traditional trial of maintaining strength after a conflict, but also a greater challenge—unification. Influential senators and congressmen demanded greater centralization in the national military command structure. Several key legislators and officers of the Army advocated the latter's assimilation of Marine Corps combat functions, in essence the dissolution of the Marine Corps. At the same time, proponents of an independent Air Force dismissed the need for naval aviation.[15]

Under growing pressure, the Navy searched for new roles and missions. Ideas of concentration and fleet battles were quickly swept aside. A dispersed, peacetime Navy would play the role of national, or perhaps international, policeman. But planners reflexively assigned the American Navy the familiar waters of the Western Atlantic and the Pacific, while cooperative allies, principally Great Britain, safeguarded the world's other seas.[16]

But a basic inconsistency existed: why maintain a strong U.S. Navy in a peaceful world dominated and policed by allies? Plans completed by the end of 1943 envisioned a Navy manned by over 800,000 officers and men (including the Marine Corps), with more than a score of aircraft carriers and an annual budget of $7 billion.[17] This was a large price tag for a police force, however well prepared. As the war ended, Navy planners remained unable to formalize a postwar posture that would guarantee their service's existence as a sizeable, balanced force.

◆ ◆ ◆

James V. Forrestal, appointed Secretary of the Navy following Frank Knox's death in April 1944, brought a new dimension to planning for the postwar era. While Knox had been a rather traditional

Secretary of the Navy James V. Forrestal in Pensacola, Florida, December 1946. (NH 54749)

secretary and one sympathetic to the concept of unification of the armed forces, Forrestal was an activist bureaucrat, an opponent of unification, a cold warrior before the advent of the Cold War, and a man open to new approaches and solutions. As early as June 1944 Forrestal implored naval officers to end their "luxury of separation" from national affairs and to take a more active and vocal role as advocates of their service.[18]

Initially, Forrestal's ideas differed little from others in the naval establishment. In a 1943 address, he spoke of the need to maintain adequate "police power . . . to curb the ruffians of the world."[19] Forrestal saw the Navy as "an instrument of national policy, an instrument usable and to be used for the purpose of peace rather than war."[20] As late as July 1945, he foresaw American naval commitments restricted primarily to the Pacific and the Western Atlantic.[21]

Forrestal's major contribution to Navy planning was his identification of the Soviet Union as the United States' most probable postwar enemy, despite its lack of a strong, blue-water navy.[22] Forrestal, the "most forceful advocate" of the new concept of national security, had a longstanding mistrust of the Soviets. As the first prominent administration figure to embrace the "Riga axioms," he labelled the Soviet government as a totalitarian dictatorship on par with Nazi Germany, and called for an American hard-line policy.[23]

Forrestal's focus on the Soviet Union, combined with his emphasis on the Navy's mission to support actively the government's foreign policy, provided Navy planners with relevant parameters.[24] Forrestal recognized the need to develop adequate plans for a postwar world in which the Navy would face internal and external threats. As Vincent Davis wrote, "Well understanding the fact that in Washington when an agency does not have its own program, other groups will usually attempt to provide one for it, he very soon began to assume an active role in leading the Navy's postwar planning."[25] Thus, while the administration continued to speak of postwar Allied harmony, the Navy, at Forrestal's direction, assumed the opposite in its planning.[26]

There followed a fall 1944 shakeup as Forrestal badgered the uniformed staffs of the Commander in Chief/Chief of Naval Operations to stimulate fresh planning under the new assumptions. In March 1945 the Navy issued Basic Post-War Plan No. 1, signed by Fleet Admiral Ernest J. King, COMINCH/CNO. Based on a memo drawn up by the staff of Admiral Richard S. Edwards, Deputy COMINCH/

CNO, the new document assumed that, having twice been involved in world wars in a quarter century, the United States would become involved in future conflicts, and that an adequate military force provided the best means to deter, or wage, such a war. Under the plan, the United States would maintain a navy strong enough to control the Pacific (six carriers) and the Western Atlantic and its approaches (three carriers), and flexible enough to move wherever needed. Planners expected the Navy to maintain its postwar strength at a level of 50,000 officers and 500,000 seamen, with a Marine Corps one-fifth as large.[27] The Navy's peacekeeping role would last only until an international organization became "fully effective." The planners thus avoided a direct clash with administration policy. They expected the United States to retain adequate worldwide bases, especially those in the Pacific, and negotiate to maintain bases around the Atlantic basin—Iceland, Greenland, the Azores and Canaries, Dakar, Liberia, Morocco, and Ascension Island.[28]

The plan demonstrated that many senior officers still found it difficult to break their prewar Pacific mindset and to consider the Soviet Union, a land power posing virtually no naval challenge to the United States, an enemy against which sea power could be applied. Even Forrestal had difficulty envisioning such an application.[29] Vice Admiral Marc A. Mitscher, in a memo sent to Forrestal in September 1945, wrote:

> The only two nations powerful enough in the near future to wage war against the United States are Russia and Great Britain. Russia now has a small Navy and a large air force. Great Britain has a medium sized Navy and air force. It is unlikely that Great Britain will attempt an aggressive war in the near future.[30]

But Mitscher nonetheless concluded that "the major portion of our Fleet should be kept in the Pacific."

The weaknesses of the new plan were widely recognized. Forrestal believed that the planners had undervalued submarines and carriers, a view many officers shared. The uncertainty surrounding the Navy's mission and the fiscal and manpower support troubled many. King, himself, had doubts about the plan and instructed Vice Admiral Harry W. Hill and Rear Admirals William H. P. Blandy and Arthur W. Radford to evaluate it.[31]

The views of the three officers differed. Radford, a strong proponent of naval aviation, recommended doubling the number of carriers. Blandy, representing the surface officers of the old "Gun Club," rejected recommendations to demobilize additional battleships instead of carriers. Hill, a former war plans officer for Commander in Chief, U.S. Fleet (CINCUS), and planner in the Office of the Chief of Naval Operations (OPNAV), proposed a balanced Navy of air, surface, subsurface, amphibious, and support forces. He judged the most likely conflict a "unilateral action against Russia," a struggle he did not consider a classical "naval war." To fight the Soviet Union, the United States needed

> a well balanced force, complete with carrier striking force, bombardment group, and an amphibious force with . . . tactical air support, UDT's [underwater demolition teams], and minesweepers, capable of effecting a landing and occupying territory against land-based air and ground opposition. There should be such a force— *well balanced in composition and complete with all units*—available for instant use in each ocean.[32]

Hill recommended the retention of more carriers and amphibious types and fewer battleships and submarines.

Hill's reaction to Basic Post-War Plan No. 1 and comments from "interested officers and officials of the Navy Department" indicated that the Navy was beginning to grapple with postwar realities. Hill alone identified the Soviet Union as the nation's most likely enemy, a foe against which the Navy must prepare to fight as much ashore as at sea. While he did not envision the United States waging war as an ally of Britain, Hill had confronted the "transoceanic" challenge. King forwarded the reports to Secretary Forrestal with recommendations for revision of the plan along the lines suggested by Hill, including a minor increase in the number of carriers on active service.[33]

Despite such attempts to formulate a postwar plan, the Navy still lacked a clearly defined strategic concept at the end of the Second World War. The service groped towards an uncertain future in search of a transoceanic policy, ignoring its own amphibious experience in the European theater. Radford spoke for many when he observed:

> I am optimistic in regard to the *possibilities* of the future insofar as the Navy is concerned. No armed service in the world today has a better technical background with which to face the dawn of the Atomic Age than the United States Navy. I am extremely pessi-

mistic as to the *actualities* of the future unless there is an immediate renaissance within the service. A change in the Naval "attitude of mind" for want of a better expression. Now or never is the time for critical and ruthless self-examination. Now is the time to eliminate any possibility of self-interest or sentiment from acts of the present or plans for the future. We must realize that the time is past when Navy recommendations on Naval matters will be accepted without question.[34]

For the U.S. Navy, the challenges of the postwar world would be as exacting as those of the war years. The battles of the Atlantic and the Pacific were over; the "battle of Washington" was about to begin.

2 · *A Prospective Enemy*

THE immediate postwar period was one of transition for the United States. The Japanese attack on Pearl Harbor and the German declaration of war in December 1941 had driven isolationists and unilateralists to the fringes of the American foreign policy spectrum. To the fore had come not practitioners of the "old diplomacy"—balance of power politics and alliance systems—but proponents of the new, embracing Progressive concepts of collective security epitomized by President Woodrow Wilson's League of Nations ideal. The Grand Alliance, seen only as a wartime necessity, would be discarded in favor of a global collective order. For the majority of the American people and the administration of President Harry S. Truman, the United Nations would be the centerpiece for a postwar system of international peace and stability. The special Anglo-American relationship would be terminated; Britain and the Soviet Union would be treated equally, lest the latter's fear of a capitalist cabal threaten postwar harmony and Soviet-American conciliation.[1]

That course, the legacy of President Franklin Delano Roosevelt, weighed heavily on the Truman administration and could not easily be reversed. Roosevelt attributed nonrecognition of the Bolshevik regime to the "Red Scare" hysteria of the post-World War I years. In the spring before the 1932 election, FDR and his advisors considered diplomatic recognition of the Soviet Union, accompanied by increased trade, as an economic measure for a depression-racked America. Adolf Hitler's accession to power in Germany in January 1933 and troubles with Japan in East Asia made a Soviet-American rapprochement seem sensible from a strategic standpoint as well. After carefully gauging domestic opinion, the Roosevelt administration moved rapidly and in November 1933 established diplomatic relations with the Soviet Union.[2]

The United States enjoyed neither the economic nor the strategic fruits of reconciliation during the years before the Second World War. In particular, the U.S. Navy's leadership resisted administration efforts to forge a closer relationship with the Soviets. Admiral William D. Leahy, Chief of Naval Operations, and others in the Navy bureaucracy obstructed implementation of plans to build warships, including a 35-knot, 60,000-ton battleship mounting 18-inch guns, for the Soviet Union.[3]

Not until the German invasion of Russia in June 1941 and the Japanese attack on Pearl Harbor that December did a purposeful relationship develop—a wartime alliance of the United States and the Soviet Union. Despite the ideological differences between the two nations, the policy of reconciliation ultimately served American security interests, as Roosevelt had foreseen in the early 1930s. Thus the Soviet-American relationship, central to the successful prosecution of the war and heavily propagandized during the conflict, held wide public support in the United States and could not easily be jettisoned by Truman.

While there were a few American officials whose belief in a continued Soviet-American relationship appears naive in retrospect, most viewed the wartime alliance as a marriage of convenience and expected Soviet and American interests to diverge in the postwar period. Roosevelt and initially Truman, whom John Lewis Gaddis has characterized as a "more dedicated Wilsonian than his predecessor," believed that this divergence of interest could be managed better through cooperation than confrontation.[4] Harry Hopkins, advisor to both presidents, understood that Soviet actions in Central and Eastern Europe in 1946 undermined the cooperative arrangement and eroded domestic support in the United States for its postwar continuation. Nevertheless, he favored continued cooperation, writing shortly before his death in 1946: "Our Russian policy must not be dictated by people who have already made up their minds that there is no possibility of working with Russians and that our interests are bound to conflict and ultimately lead to war. From my point of view, that is an untenable position and can but lead to disaster."[5]

But those who did not see the choice as one between concession and war believed that firmness would promote Soviet-American cooperation and peace.[6] Forrestal, his perceptions of Russian actions and motivations reinforced by the reports and opinions of Ambassador Averell Harriman in Moscow and other American diplomats, favored a "showdown" with the Soviets.[7]

While Forrestal's views were widely shared within the Navy, administration policy nevertheless remained in force.[8] A December 1945 naval intelligence overview of the world situation, for example, considered the Soviet Union's fears of the West "half-justified." The report concluded that American options were limited: either total war or continued cooperation, the latter to be accomplished through the elimination of "misunderstanding and suspicion."[9]

Accordingly, the Navy did not immediately focus on the Soviet Union after the war. Demobilization, the abrupt end of the war in the Pacific, and the deteriorating situation in China dominated events.[10] A confidential memo of 8 January 1946 listed the primary tasks of the Atlantic and Pacific fleets as promotion of the "foreign policy of the United States," support of "the occupation forces in Europe and the Western Pacific," demobilization, training, and achievement of readiness "for limited hostile operations."[11] The Atlantic Fleet was further instructed "to maintain command of the Western part of the North and South Atlantic Ocean and approaches thereto, and be ready to move promptly and in effective force to any part of the world in support of our national policies."[12]

Operational plans for American naval forces in European waters focused primarily on demobilization and support of occupation forces in Western Europe, but not on a naval role in the conduct of American foreign policy. Vice Admiral Bernhard H. Bieri, who relieved Rear Admiral Jules James as Commander U.S. Naval Forces, Mediterranean (COMNAVMED), noted in an interview: "I never did receive from anyone a statement of our policy in connection with any government in the Mediterranean, or bordering the Mediterranean."[13]

◆ ◆ ◆

As a key figure in reshaping the administration's policy towards the Soviet Union and in preparing the Navy to support that policy, Secretary of the Navy Forrestal deserves the credit and attention given him by historians over the last four decades. Robert Greenhalgh Albion was certainly justified when he ranked Forrestal as one of the Navy's three greatest secretaries.[14] In the postwar period, Forrestal was the spokesman for a Navy Department/OPNAV partnership committed to the support of the nation's foreign policy and preparation for hostilities.[15] Unfortunately, the historic invisibility of the "Blue Suiters," senior veteran naval officers, persisted because of the classified nature of their work, the anonymity that usually surrounded their endeavors, and the unusually high profile of Secretary Forrestal.[16]

Forrestal and the uniformed Navy, once freed from the immediate task of defeating the Axis powers, quickly began to prepare and plan for a possible crisis or war with the Soviet Union. During a 19 September 1945 appearance before Congress, Forrestal stressed the need for a large, powerful, postwar Navy to defend the Continental United States, the Western Hemisphere, and the Pacific. "The outstanding lesson of the past quarter century," he observed, "is that the means to wage war must be in the hands of those who hate war. The United States should remain strong."[17]

But why such a large Navy? A sympathetic congressman, James W. Mott, quoting Forrestal's own statement on a strong Navy "for the maintenance of peace," twice pressed the secretary to confirm that the fleet could conceivably be used against former allies. In each instance, Forrestal declined to answer in the affirmative. Refusing to yield, Mott asked a third time:

> One final question. The proposal to maintain this great fleet, a fleet probably greater than that of all the navies of the world combined, is not simply based on the possibility that we might have some trouble with nations in the future that we have already conquered. Is not the purpose of this fleet to have one stronger than any other power or any other combination of powers, no matter who they are, that they can bring against us in the event that unfortunate eventuality should ever arise?

Forrestal at last replied, "That is my own personal view, Mr. Mott."[18]

Fleet Admiral King, who shared Forrestal's views on the Soviet threat and a strong Navy, also fielded Congressman Mott's queries. In his prepared text, King had written of the American "naval force and effort which will be required in connection with the positive insurance that Japan maintains the peace." But in his testimony, King al-

tered that passage to read "insurance that Japan or anyone else maintains the peace." Mott requested a clarification. Should the Congress
take the prepared or spoken text as the CNO's statement? When
King stood by the latter, Mott asked, "What you said stands—that
you want a Navy big enough to require Japan and everyone else to
maintain the peace?" King replied in the affirmative, to which Mott
responded, "I am glad to hear that."[19] Unwilling publicly to appear in
conflict with administration policy, Forrestal and King were under-
standably reticent about naming the Soviet Union as the greatest
threat to peace. But the Secretary of the Navy was busily filling his
diary with excerpts of top secret reports that reinforced his fear and
distrust of the Soviets.[20]

While Forrestal testified before Congress, the Joint Staff Planners
(JPS) presented a planning paper, JCS 1518, prepared on "their own
initiative," to the Joint Chiefs of Staff. Entitled "Strategic Concept
and Plan for the Employment of United States Armed Forces," the
study focused on a "conflict with a major power over an issue vital to
the interests of the United States, not capable of a solution by the
United Nations Organization."[21] The document assumed that such a
war would pit the United States and Great Britain against the Soviet
Union, most likely after a "demonstration of intent" to overrun
Western Europe or China. The main objective of the draft plan was
to keep "a prospective enemy at the maximum possible distance, and
conversely to project our own advance bases into areas well removed
from the United States. . . . The overall effect is to enlarge our strategic frontier." The study recommended forward basing of forces, especially sea and air, and alluded to an American preemptive strike,
should a Soviet attack appear imminent. Further, the document called
for "a rapid and effective series of initial operations, exploiting special weapons and the great mobility of airborne and seaborne forces,
to destroy or disrupt the more dangerous enemy means of action or
counter-action, to blockade, to bombard and to initiate the destruction of his war making capacity."[22]

Admiral King reviewed the draft and enclosed a memo to the secretary of the Joint Chiefs suggesting that since "no nation can effectively carry on war against the United States without an adequate
Navy and Merchant Marine, it appears to me that the over-all concept should require the early destruction of those forces." As a result
of the CNO's observation, the planning paper was amended to in-

Fleet Admirals Ernest J. King (*left*) and Chester W. Nimitz with Secretary Forrestal after the announcement, on 21 November 1945, that Nimitz will replace King as Chief of Naval Operations. (80-G-701553)

clude an "early destruction of his [the Soviet's] naval forces and shipping without which he would be unable effectively to support his overseas bases or land forces on our shores."[23]

Less than a fortnight after the Japanese surrender, the JPS had identified the Soviet Union as a major antagonist and Great Britain as a probable ally. The Navy, through the insistence of King, had stressed the importance of forward offensive operations in the postwar world. But the JPS study, accepted on 9 October by the JCS, was only a beginning. Formal and sophisticated military planning had yet to begin; a system of State Department/military coordination remained to be established; and national interests had to be clarified by the administration.

Definition, coordination, and planning took a major step forward on 6 March 1946. Secretary of State James F. Byrnes, with President Truman's approval, urgently requested of the JCS "an appraisal from the military point of view" of the direct impact on U.S. national security (or the indirect effect through pressure on the British Commonwealth) of meeting "in whole or in part" Soviet demands in the eastern Mediterranean.[24] Simultaneously, the State Department announced that the battleship *Missouri* (BB-63) would transport to Istanbul the remains of the former Turkish ambassador to the United States. The day before, Winston S. Churchill, with the foreknowledge of Truman, Byrnes, and Fleet Admiral Leahy, Chief of the Joint Chiefs of Staff, had delivered his famous "Iron Curtain" speech in Fulton, Missouri. The administration began to prepare the ground for a harder line towards the Soviet Union.[25]

On 10 March 1946 the JPS, to whom the Byrnes request had been forwarded, presented its report to the Joint Chiefs. The JPS concluded that Soviet demands in the eastern Mediterranean posed such a threat to Britain's imperial position that the once-mighty empire would be forced either to fight or surrender her station as a world power. The JPS report observed that Britain's "defeat or disintegration . . . would eliminate from Eurasia the last bulwark of resistance between the United States and Soviet expansion. . . . Militarily, our present position as a world power is of necessity closely interwoven with that of Great Britain." It concluded that "acquiescence by [the United States], in whole or in part, to these Soviet demands, although they do not constitute a direct threat, will definitely impair our national security by weakening the British position as a world power and reducing the effectiveness of the United Nations."

The Joint Staff Planners recommended that the JCS request from the Secretary of State "a political estimate of Russia and, so far as possible, an outline of future U.S. policy with reference to Russia, and implementing action for that policy requiring plans and preparations by the armed forces."[26] The latter request was sent to the State-War-Navy Coordinating Committee (SWNCC) and to Secretary Byrnes on 13 March.[27]

On 5 April the State Department replied to this request, referring the JCS to George F. Kennan's "Long Telegram" of 22 February, one of the foundation documents of containment, for the sources of Soviet conduct. But the diplomats were unable to visualize just how to coordinate the peacetime politico-military efforts of the United States to meet the Soviet challenge, as the JPS had requested. The memorandum suggested that the United States use "diplomatic means" to demonstrate its resolve until the Soviets actually seized regions; then their armies would be countered "by the naval, amphibious, and air power of the U.S. and its potential allies." Even in this case, the diplomats suggested that the American effort be carried out under United Nations' auspices.[28]

Once again on their own initiative, the joint planners were already at work preparing a military analysis. On 11 April they presented to the JCS an "Estimate Based on Assumptions of Occurrences of Major Hostilities." The JPS concluded that in a major war pitting the Soviet Union against Great Britain and the United States, the Soviets would overrun most of western continental Europe, European Turkey, Iran, Iraq, possibly the Suez Canal, Korea, Manchuria, and North China. In this scenario, the first American military task would be the evacuation of occupation forces. The Navy would attempt to deny the Soviets control of the Mediterranean, the Yellow Sea, and the Sea of Japan, while securing the British Isles, Iceland, Greenland, the Aleutians, and Japan from attack. From bases in the Far East, Britain, and the Middle East, the allies would wage a strategic air offensive against the Soviet heartland. The American planners hoped that a lodgement could be retained somewhere on the continent, most likely in Scandinavia, Spain, or Italy. The only land area contiguous to the Soviet Union and its East European positions where resistance seemed worthwhile was the eastern Mediterranean and the Middle East.[29]

The disparity in strength between the land forces of the West and those of the Soviet Union forced a reliance in this and later American military estimates on strategic air attack, conventional or atomic. The objective of the air offensive would be to destroy Soviet industrial war-making potential and sea power; to safeguard key island bases, such as Britain and Japan; and to apply power in areas where poor lines of communication restricted the use of Soviet ground forces, for example, in the Mediterranean. American strategic focus in the Mediterranean and other regions on the European periphery marked a reversal of the strategy employed during the Second World War.[30]

The call for closer cooperation with Great Britain also reversed wartime intentions to treat all nations equally in the postwar world. Forrestal saw Great Britain, whose leaders seemed more aware of the Russian peril, as an ally in an inevitable struggle with the Soviet Union.[31] He believed that the strong Anglo-American alliance should continue to function after the war. Nonetheless, in August 1945 he queried Assistant Secretary of War John McCloy on the postwar fate of the Combined Chiefs of Staff (CCS), only to find the Army content to see the CCS terminated.[32] In fact, at the end of the war President Truman allowed most of the wartime bodies to atrophy and die. By October 1945, lend-lease to Britain and the work of other wartime Anglo-American combined boards had been halted. Planning by the Combined Chiefs of Staff proceeded only in relation to postwar occupation duties and demobilization.[33]

The British, like the Americans, planned for the peace in mid-war. Just as euphoria over Napoleon's 1812 defeat in Russia gave way to fear over what the triumphant Russians might do in Europe, in 1943 British planners demonstrated a similar concern.[34] As early as the fall of that year the Post-Hostilities Planning Committee (PHPC), on which both the Foreign Office and the Chiefs of Staff (COS) were represented, considered possible Soviet demands for revision of the Montreux Convention regarding use of the Turkish Straits. A June 1944 PHPC report reviewed the Soviet threat to British interests in the Middle East. If the Soviets could not be placated diplomatically, the report recommended that Britain develop secure military and political positions in Greece and Turkey, foster greater collaboration with other Western European countries, and secure the cooperation of the United States to support British objectives. In July the planners considered possible reliance on a revived Germany. They recommended a policy that encouraged the development of American interests in Europe and the Middle East, and convinced the Americans to keep their forces in Europe after the war.[35]

The Post-Hostilities Planning Committee's positions were at odds with the policy of the British government, which was as committed as its American counterpart to continued cooperation with the Soviet Union. Foreign Minister Anthony Eden and his staff did not reject the views of the committee, although they insisted that its recommendations be kept quiet, lest they enrage the Soviets, not to mention those Europeans living under German occupation. Since Soviet spy Donald Maclean was one of the men privy to the committee's reports, Stalin undoubtedly was aware of the nature of Britain's wartime planning.[36]

American officials, such as Vice Admiral Bieri, temporarily detached during the summer of 1944 from King's COMINCH/CNO staff and assigned to Supreme Headquarters, Allied Expeditionary Force, Europe (SHAEF), were aware of the advanced state of British planning for the postwar world. In a letter to Commander U.S. Naval Forces, Europe, Admiral Harold R. Stark, Bieri noted that the British recognized their relative weakness vis-à-vis the Soviet Union and the

United States and expected the latter to maintain naval forces in European waters at war's end. This troubled Bieri, for he knew that American naval officers intended to redirect the American effort to the Pacific with Germany's final defeat and to leave Europe to the Royal Navy.[37]

After the war, many senior American diplomats in Europe were aware not only of possible problems with the Soviets but also of British military, economic, and social exhaustion. They saw the need for an increased American role in Europe, especially in the Mediterranean and the Middle East. Lincoln MacVeagh, American ambassador to the Greek government in exile, warned President Roosevelt in the spring of 1944 that he expected to see the Soviets and the British resume the old "diplomatic game" in the Balkans, Eastern Europe, and the Middle East.[38] In the fall, MacVeagh wrote:

> Russian interests are clearly tending to cross with Britain's in this region even now. Nor is this all. Evidence is equally plain right here of Britain's inability to defend alone her Empire against powerful pressure under conditions of modern war. I doubt if in any other part of the world it can appear so clearly as here,—along its principal artery,—that, militarily speaking, the British Empire is anachronistic, perfect for the eighteenth century, impossible for the twentieth. Every day brings its evidence of weakness and dispersion, of consequent opportunism, and dependence on America's nucleated strength. No one, I feel, can keep his eyes and ears open here [Cairo] and fail to believe that the future maintenance of the Empire depends on how far England consents to frame her foreign policy in agreement with Washington, and how far in our turn we realize where that Empire, so important to our own security, is most immediately menaced.[39]

In the course of the Second World War, American diplomats began to perceive an American stake in an area long under contention. Greece, Turkey, and Iran became recognizable outposts—the Northern Tier—a buffer against aggression from the north. A shared perception of threatened Western security in this region gradually overshadowed American distaste for British imperial policy.[40]

Nevertheless, during and immediately after the war the Roosevelt and Truman administrations were unmoved by, if not unaware of, probable Soviet actions and British incapacity to resist. The Mediterranean and the Middle East were British theaters of little concern to most Americans.[41] American disinterest in the Mediterranean is evident in the debates over European strategy.[42] The British viewed the theater as the lifeline of the Empire. The Americans considered the region a backwater of marginal importance. The U.S. Army, especially General George C. Marshall, focused on northwest Europe. If some American naval officers better understood the underlying philosophy of the British view, their own focus remained, nonetheless, on the Pacific.

Churchill had spent the war years not only struggling unsuccessfully with the Americans over strategic questions but also attempting to secure continued cooperation in the postwar world. In a 1943 Harvard address, delivered shortly after the Quebec Conference, Churchill sounded out the Americans on the question of the postwar Anglo-American relationship, but was disappointed by the response. The prime minister reminded his audience: "The price of greatness is responsibility. . . . One cannot rise to be in many ways the leading community in the civilized world without being involved in its problems, without being convulsed by its agonies and inspired by its causes."[43] He suggested "common citizenship" for the people of the two nations. But the Americans remained uncommitted. At Quebec, Harry Hopkins carried with him a military estimate that accurately forecast the British postwar position.

> Russia's post-war position in Europe will be a dominant one. With Germany crushed, there is no power in Europe to oppose her tremendous military forces. It is true that Great Britain is building up a position in the Mediterranean vis-à-vis Russia that she may find useful in balancing power in Europe. However, even here she may not be able to oppose Russia unless she is otherwise supported.

But the appreciation did not call for American support of Britain. Instead, it noted, "since without question [the Soviet Union] will dominate Europe on the defeat of the Axis, it is even more essential to develop and maintain the most friendly relations with Russia." The reasoning was simple: lack of American interest in European postwar affairs and an immediate concern with the Pacific theater. *"The most important factor the United States has to consider in relation to Russia is the prosecution of the war in the Pacific."*[44] The study suggested:

> We now have a number of United States representatives in contact with Russian representatives who do not trust Russia and who

do not follow a national policy of the "good neighbor and a sincere friend" to Russia. . . . These should either be replaced or they should be required to pledge loyal support to the above policy. . . . It is suspected that Russia feels England has established a position of such close relationship to America that it is quite difficult for us to treat Russia and England on a basis of equality. It is believed to be important that we maintain a reasonably independent position so that we can treat both of these countries as good neighbors and sincere friends and give fair consideration to the positions, aims and aspirations of both.[45]

While most Americans were willing to accept the international responsibilities that came with "greatness," they were not prepared in 1943, nor immediately after the war, to join with Britain in securing Europe.

Even as the totality of the Allied victory during the Second World War eliminated the Navy's primary reason for existence, it ended the main rationale for Soviet-American conciliation and cooperation. To many Americans, the actions in Central and Eastern Europe of the Soviets reflected justifiable concern for security, although Communist heavy handedness eroded much of the reservoir of Western goodwill built up during the war.[46] But Soviet demands in the Mediterranean and the Middle East directly threatened the imperial and maritime positions of Great Britain. American interest in the defense of Britain's global position, evident even in the prewar years, grew stronger during the war and continued in its wake. Furthermore, the Soviet demands posed a more traditional maritime challenge in areas peripheral to the Soviet Union. There, the West's, particularly the United States', strong suits—naval and air power—could come into play. As a result, in the spring of 1946 the Joint Chiefs of Staff began to shape a maritime-based strategy in which the Navy would play a leading role and discover for itself a new *raison d'être.*

3 · *Fathering a Maritime Strategy*

EARLY in 1946 the Navy redirected its attention to Europe. Secretary Forrestal instructed American naval forces to steam "in any waters in any part of the globe" so as not to cause "excitement or speculation" when crisis deployments were required. During this period, one is hard pressed to find an area of Europe, other than the Soviet Union itself, that did not receive a visit from a U.S. naval vessel, conducting a "midshipmen" or "reservist" cruise.[1] Coordinating this military-diplomatic effort was the Navy's former wartime London headquarters, U.S. Naval Forces, Europe, under the command of Vice Admiral Richard L. Conolly.[2]

The Mediterranean was central to the new American naval policy. In January 1946 the Navy prepared "a heavy striking force" to be kept in *"constant readiness for offensive operations,"* ostensibly in the Eastern Atlantic or Caribbean.[3] Fleet Admiral Chester W. Nimitz, Chief of Naval Operations, ordered Vice Admiral Mitscher, one of the Navy's most skilled and experienced combat commanders, to form a staff for the new Eighth Fleet. But the real reason for the action was to prepare a force for deployment to the Mediterranean during a crisis. When Captain Arleigh A. Burke was called to serve as Mitscher's chief of staff, he questioned why the Eighth Fleet was being established. Mitscher replied, "to create a task force to go to the Mediterranean within three months, ready for combat."[4]

While the initiative appears to have been Forrestal's, Vice Admiral Forrest P. Sherman, Deputy Chief of Naval Operations (DCNO) for Operations (OP-03), was the moving force behind the effort in OPNAV.[5] Sherman also proposed using *Missouri,* accompanied by ships from Mitscher's newly formed command, for the highly pub-

The battleship *Missouri* off Istanbul, Turkey, in April 1946, flanked by the destroyer *Power,* and the Turkish battle cruiser *Yavuz,* the former German *Goeben.* (80-G-366179)

Fleet Admirals Nimitz and William D. Leahy, President Harry S. Truman, and Vice Admiral Marc A. Mitscher on the bridge of the aircraft carrier *Franklin D. Roosevelt,* flagship of the Eighth Fleet, during maneuvers off the Virginia Capes on 24 April 1946. (80-G-702511)

Missouri at anchor in Phaleron Bay, Greece, in April 1946. (80-G-K-9343)

licized cruise to Turkey, although the idea itself originated with Admiral Richmond Kelly Turner.[6] After giving tentative approval to Forrestal's plan for use of the Eighth Fleet in the Mediterranean, Truman and Byrnes decided that a less formidable display of American naval strength in European waters was appropriate.[7]

While the Eighth Fleet never made it to the Mediterranean, its senior officers, accompanied by Forrest Sherman, did. They toured Europe in the summer of 1946. During a meeting with Britain's First Sea Lord and Chief of the Naval Staff, Admiral of the Fleet Lord Cunningham of Hyndhope, the American party learned of Britain's "inability to support their whole Mediterranean forces any more." If the Soviets were to be contained, Britain would need "help from the United States in Europe."[8]

By mid-1946 American naval leaders had identified the Soviet Union as the nation's major antagonist and recognized that the burden of meeting the Russian challenge would fall mainly on the United States. The Navy determined to meet that challenge as far forward as possible—in the European and Pacific maritime approaches to the Soviet Union. OPNAV slowed the withdrawal of forces from the Western Pacific and planned for a stronger commitment in the Mediterranean, a region where only a year before the Navy had shown virtually no interest.[9]

The Navy's forward posture conformed to the planning being conducted at the highest levels of the U.S. defense establishment. On 14 December 1945, formal, official planning for a war with the Soviet

Union began at the JCS level. The Joint War Plans Committee initiated a series of studies, codenamed Pincher, to support the development of a joint strategic war plan to "Reduce the Military and Political Capabilities of the U.S.S.R. to the extent necessary to.deny to the Soviets the ability to impose their will upon other major powers in order to prevent world domination by the U.S.S.R." [10]

Vice Admiral Sherman crafted the naval component of the nation's new strategic concept. At a 6 June 1946 conference with his Strategic Plans Division (OP-30) staff Sherman emphasized that a well-developed Pincher plan was "the most pressing business of OP-30." [11] The purpose of the meeting was to ensure that Sherman's concept of a Pincher war became the Navy's position in the service and joint planning processes. [12]

The admiral believed that a Soviet-American conflict would be a global, protracted war. Initially, the United States would find itself on the strategic defensive. The Navy's missions in this early stage were many. Naval forces would support the operations of American occupation forces overseas, covering the Dunkirk-like evacuations that the Army had planned for northern and southern Europe, North China, and the Korean peninsula. The Navy would defend overseas allies and forward bases in Iceland, the Azores, the British Isles, the Suez-Cairo area, the Aleutians, Japan, the Ryukyus, and the Philippines. The Navy would keep the sea lines of communication (SLOCs) open to these forward bases by maintaining control of the North Atlantic, the Mediterranean, and the Western Pacific.

These missions necessitated forward, offensive, conventional operations. Sherman believed that, given the "limited supply of atomic bombs," the United States would have to rely on conventional forces during the initial stages of the war. In the Pacific, a carrier task force would "wipe up the Russian Fleet Bases." In European waters, where all but a single carrier task force would ultimately be concentrated, American naval operations would focus on the eastern Mediterranean in an attempt to keep Turkey in the war. American submarines would attack Soviet surface and subsurface targets at sea. Antisubmarine Warfare (ASW) ships and aircraft would contain the Soviet submarine menace, already perceived as the major threat. The Soviet surface threat was considered negligible. As soon as possible, American strategic bombers would launch air attacks on the U.S.S.R. from land bases secured by the Navy's control of the sea.

Sherman recommended that his planners "resist pressure to get up

Midway's flight deck during Operation Frostbite in Davis Strait off
Greenland, March 1946.

into the ice" of the Arctic should war come within the next three
years. In March 1946, the Navy had conducted Operation Frostbite to
test "the capabilities and limitations of the CVB type [*Midway*-class
carriers] under severe cold and heavy weather conditions" in the
Arctic. The report of Commander Carrier Division One concluded
that "cold weather operations with aircraft carriers in the sub-arctic
regions are feasible and can be conducted without major deviation
from established procedures . . . [although] limitations imposed by
cold weather tend to restrict and slow down the tempo of operations." Further studies, many already planned, and the digestion of
recommendations and lessons learned were needed. For the moment, Sherman believed that carriers, especially the newest CVBs,
could be better used elsewhere.[1] His decision to avoid, temporarily,
major operations in the Arctic marks a major difference between the
Navy's strategy of 1946–1947 and its Maritime Strategy of the 1980s.

The ASW problem was central to Sherman's strategy and was "assigned a priority equal to that for the Atomic Bomb Tests" by Nimitz.
The revolution in submarine warfare heralded by German technological developments late in the war was the theme of a June 1946
conference attended by Sherman. Rear Admiral Jerauld Wright con-

cluded that the snorkel, a breathing device that allowed a submarine to run submerged while using its high-speed diesel engines, reduced the ASW efficiency of aircraft, the premier threat to submarines, by 95 percent. Exercises conducted with the two Type XXI U-boats acquired by the United States at the end of the war revealed that German advances rendered obsolescent the Allied ASW technology and tactics that won the battle of the Atlantic. High speed and silent running made the Type XXIs extremely difficult to counter without new technology and tactics. Since the Soviets had overrun many of the U-boat production, assembly, and training sites in eastern Germany, and had received other German submarines as reparations, American naval leaders anticipated a Type XXI assault on Allied SLOCs in a future war. To Sherman, the solution to the problem was obvious: "As you know, the strategic counter to this sort of thing is high emphasis on attack at the sources of the trouble."[14]

The record of offensive ASW operations during the Second World War was mixed. During the early stages of the battle of the Atlantic, Allied navies relied on defense—the escorted convoy. This measure reduced the effectiveness of the U-boats by late 1942, but did not inflict heavy losses on the attacking submarine force. The official British history of wartime operational research noted, "It was therefore essential for their final defeat that aggressive operations should be made successful."[15] The most notable offensive operation of the campaign was the effort against U-boats transiting the Bay of Biscay off France and Spain during 1942 and 1943. This offensive, combined with German failure in the mid-Atlantic convoy battles of the spring of 1943, inflicted upon the U-Waffe a decisive defeat.[16] The Allied strategic bombing offensive against German U-boat bases, on the other hand, was a notable failure.

Sherman's willingness to make attack at the source the centerpiece of the Navy's planning did not ignore the lessons of the past war.[17] The Navy had learned in the Pacific that precision strikes on bases bore more favorable results than high altitude area attacks. And, unlike U-boat pens, Soviet submarine bases were not hardened. Even if the bases were eventually hardened, as might be expected, the Navy was developing a heavy attack plane capable of carrying large conventional and atomic bombs suitable for strikes on such targets. A supercarrier in the early planning stage would serve as a platform for this next, heavier generation of carrier aircraft. Given the inability of

Admiral Nimitz and Vice Admiral Forrest P. Sherman inspect a captured German Type XXI U-boat on 11 May 1946. (NH 58138)

defensive measures to cope with the Type XXI, the Navy had little
choice but to opt for the offensive.

⟨At Sherman's prompting, Navy planners accorded high priority to
offensive operations, an emphasis supported by contemporary stud-
ies⟩ Destruction of airfields, assembly depots, factories, shipyards,
and submarine bases, and the seizure of critical ports, harbors, and
base sites offered the best method of protecting shipping from Soviet
submarines and land-based aircraft. Aerial bombardment and offensive mining by aircraft, submarines, and surface vessels would achieve
these objectives. Carrier operations in the Mediterranean, the North
Sea, ultimately the Barents Sea, and the Sea of Japan would support
the campaign, in cooperation with the Air Force.[18] Submarines would
also play an offensive role by hunting down their Soviet counterparts.

The U.S. Navy was confident that its carrier groups could operate
within range of Soviet air power. In testimony before Congress in
May 1945, Forrestal observed that the final stage of the Pacific con-

flict was a struggle, "unique in the history of war," between sea and land-based air power.[19] Sherman, an aviator and Nimitz's wartime deputy chief of staff for plans, was prepared to send the carriers into "harm's way" should a Soviet-American war erupt.

A March 1947 analysis of carrier offensive capabilities, Naval Strategic Planning Study (NSPS) 3 supported the service's faith in its air arm.[20] Based on the Navy's World War II experiences in the Pacific, the study concluded that carriers could operate effectively in the face of quantitatively superior Soviet air power. The Pacific war demonstrated that mobility, concentration, and surprise were the keys to successful carrier operations. Naval air accounted for 68 percent of the Japanese planes destroyed during the Philippines campaign, most of them on the ground. Land-based aircraft were less effective. Carrier planes carried a lighter bomb load but delivered ordnance with greater precision than land-based bombers. In addition, lack of forward air bases would characterize a Soviet-American war, just as it had the Japanese-American struggle.[21] The Navy planners concluded:

> Therefore carrier air power, operating from the highly mobile, self-defending, and self-sustaining bases embodied in the carrier attack force, is the only weapon in the possession of the U.S. which can deliver early and effective attacks against Russian air power and selected shore objectives in the initial stages of a Russo-American conflict.

NSPS 3 called for Pacific Fleet carrier operations in the Sea of Okhotsk, the Yellow Sea, and the Sea of Japan, and Atlantic Fleet operations in the Mediterranean. The planners considered a carrier offensive in the Arctic, Soviet strength and the weather permitting, but ruled out operations in the confined Baltic. The plan's appendices depicted possible operations in the Mediterranean and included maps of the entire Soviet Union, showing the area within range of carrier-based planes.[22]

Noticeably absent from NSPS 3 was a major Navy role in the strategic bombing campaign that planners of all services recognized would be central to an American effort to destroy the Soviet industrial infrastructure in a protracted war. Navy planners concluded that the Air Force was best suited to conduct a strategic bombing campaign, although a "large" carrier could launch an aircraft carrying a heavy bomb, conventional or atomic, on a long-range mission. Such an option, they expected, would be considered if no other force was available or "surprise" was desired. The planners saw carrier air power assisting an Air Force strategic bombing campaign by engaging and destroying enemy fighter strength around the periphery of the Soviet Union. At this stage in the postwar period, with the supply of atomic bombs limited and delivery systems in their infancy, a cooperative, primarily conventional strategic warfare campaign made sense.

But suppression of Soviet air defenses was not a mission the Air Force was asking the Navy to perform, or considered necessary. Many in the new American air arm believed that the Navy had the lessons of the Pacific War backward—the long-range heavy bombers, the B-29s, had suppressed Japanese tactical air power, thereby making the Navy's successes possible. The Air Force opposed any intrusion into what it saw as its realm—strategic bombing.[23]

Despite NSPS 3's favorable view of potential carrier operations in the Arctic, the Mediterranean remained the principal theater for Navy planners, as it was for the JCS and the civilian leaders of the executive branch who secured aid for Greece and Turkey under the Truman Doctrine. In April 1947 the JCS completed a study on the availability of forces for an emergency short of war and identified Palestine as the most suitable area for an American base of operations in the eastern Mediterranean.[24] In an August 1947 study of Mediterranean base sites, the Navy chose a site on the southern shore for the operation of a large wartime fleet. The study assumed that the Soviets would overrun most of the northern littoral and that British bases in the Mediterranean would be fully committed to the Royal Navy.[25]

The American diplomatic commitment to Iran and recognition of the importance of the region's oil increased American interest in the Middle East. Not only the eastern Mediterranean but also the Persian Gulf began to figure prominently in the Navy's plans.[26] If war broke out, a Pacific Fleet carrier-amphibious force would steam to Bahrain in the Persian Gulf where the force would come under the command of U.S. Naval Forces, Eastern Atlantic and Mediterranean (CINCNELM).[27]

The planned dispatch of a Pacific Fleet task group to the Persian Gulf demonstrated that a relative balance between the resources committed to the two oceans in the Navy's early plans and the peacetime deployments outlined in the Navy's Basic Establishment Plans had yielded to a European focus.[28] Sherman relegated the Pacific to a secondary status. All but a single-carrier task force would sortie from the Pacific in wartime. Combat-proven Pacific command teams, Mitscher and Burke for example, were reassigned to the Atlantic. The three *Midway*-class CVBs were kept in the Atlantic, even during the Korean conflict. As JCS and Navy strategic plans evolved during 1947, the Pacific's decline became official.[29]

Despite fewer resources, the Navy's plans for war in the Pacific remained as true to Sherman's strategic concept of offensive warfare as those for the Atlantic theater. To achieve the goals outlined for him by the JCS, Vice Admiral Louis E. Denfeld, Commander in Chief, Pacific (CINCPAC), oversaw the planning for a fast carrier task force operation against Soviet bases in the Kurile Islands and on the Kamchatka Peninsula to support the general destruction of "any vital elements of enemy power located within effective operating range of our bases in the PACIFIC."[30]

◆ ◆ ◆

Early in 1947 Sherman confidently unveiled his service's developing plan for a future war. The Navy's chief strategist gave top secret presentations to Truman (14 January 1947), select senators (23 January 1947), the House Armed Services Committee (18 February 1947), and the Senate Armed Services Committee (5 March 1947) (see Appendix).[31] Sherman's vision of a war with the Soviets followed the outline given to his OP-30 staff the previous June. The United States and its allies would adopt the strategic defensive early in the war. The Navy would "assume the offensive immediately in order to secure our own sea communications, support our forces overseas, disrupt enemy operations, and force dissipation of enemy strength." Carrier task forces would strike targets, at sea and ashore, in the Soviet Far East and on the flanks of the Soviet advance in Norway, northwest Germany, and, most importantly to Sherman, in the Mediterranean. Submarines would conduct forward operations in the northeastern Pacific and in the White, Baltic, and Black Seas. Amphibious forces would reinforce threatened forward positions, seize new ones, and eventually open the Dardanelles.

In Sherman's presentation the Navy had a maritime strategy, a clearly stated strategic concept, as defined seven years later by Samuel Huntington, and an organizational structure to support its implementation. Nevertheless, a third critical element—public support—

eluded the Navy. When Sherman presented a revised version of his talk to the President's Advisory Committee on the Merchant Marine on 29 April 1947, committee member James B. Black complained about restrictions on its dissemination: "This naval security. The whole problem is TOP SECRET; has to be kept quiet. It is very difficult to 'sell' a subject you can't talk about except for just a figure or two." Sherman responded that the Navy was at work on a declassified version, but admitted that he didn't want the subject of his presentation "to get into the papers."[32] A veil of secrecy continued to surround the Navy's initial postwar strategy, unlike the public exposure the Maritime Strategy receives.[33]

The framework of Sherman's strategic presentation of early 1947, especially its emphasis on forward offensive operations, is strikingly similar to the Maritime Strategy briefings conducted by the Navy in the 1980s.[34] Sherman outlined a strategy for control of the seas by a nation whose means of conventional resistance lay with the Navy and whose strategic strength was tied to forward bases.[35]

A major difference between the Navy's initial postwar strategy and its current strategy is the focus of the former on operations in the Mediterranean, and not the far north. Nevertheless, Sherman believed that, while surface and carrier operations in the Arctic were as yet not planned,

> with the passage of time and the expected development of aircraft and airborne missiles, the importance of the northern approaches to the United States will increase. We anticipate that naval forces will be called on to operate in the Arctic regions to seize and support bases for our air forces, and to prevent the use of Arctic regions as bases for attack against us. For that reason we are grasping every opportunity to increase our skill in cold weather operations and to improve our material for such service.[36]

Sherman and other Navy planners also dismissed the Russian surface fleet as inconsequential, something few American admirals of the 1980s would do. Sherman noted in his presentation that the Soviet Navy's "700 to 800 ships and craft" were "of low combat value except for submarines and motor torpedo boats."[37] He foresaw that "except for a submarine force, the Soviets" would "not be able to create an effective high seas naval force with offensive capabilities for many years." The Soviet Navy of the 1980s possesses the offensive and seagoing attributes that its 1940s predecessor lacked. In 1947 the

Navy estimated that the Soviets had 118 principal surface combatants, while the Americans had 180. Forty years later, the Soviets have 269; the United States, 222. But in the 1980s, the U.S. Navy can expect to fight alongside several significant European and Asian navies, whereas in 1947 only the rapidly declining Royal Navy, with 81 principal surface ships, was a likely maritime ally.[38]

(A careful reading of the literature on the Maritime Strategy of the 1980s reveals that the ASW problem—the threat from Soviet submarines—remains the U.S. Navy's primary concern, followed by the threat from Soviet attack aircraft. The Navy still considers the Russian surface force a tertiary naval threat, despite its progress in the 1970s and 1980s. Many U.S. naval officers worry that the Soviets will keep their surface fleet close to home in wartime and not contest American control of the high seas.)

◆ ◆ ◆

Forrest Sherman guided the development of United States naval strategy during his 1946–1947 tenure as DCNO (Operations). He gave concrete expression to Forrestal's strategic musings. Sherman's proposals for a balanced, prepared force capable of playing a global role in both peace and war gave short and long-term shape to the Navy's plans. Always present was the call for early, forward, offensive operations. The strategic plans, in turn, determined how operational commands would carry out those tasks assigned to them by the JCS and how Navy staffs would draw up programs for the future, plans for mobilization, and budget requests for Congress. By 1948 the Navy at last had a clearly defined postwar strategy—a maritime strategy.[39]

(Sherman's mid-1946 exposition shaped the Navy's postwar planning into the mid-1950s. The foundations of that strategy were the geopolitical necessities of any war with the Soviet Union, a perceived gap between antisubmarine warfare capabilities and new submarine designs, a belief in the ability of carriers to operate within range of enemy land-based aircraft, and an awareness that European waters, especially those of the Mediterranean and the Middle East, had replaced the Pacific as the main theater of operations. Over the following year and a half, the OP-30 staff produced studies and plans that, in keeping with Sherman's concepts, provided the basis for the naval contribution to the national strategic plans of the JCS and the operational plans of the various theater commanders of the Navy.

4 · A Strategy Challenged

EARLY in 1948, Vice Admiral Sherman flew to the Mediterranean to take command of what would soon become the Sixth Task Fleet.[1] Sherman had guided the development of a maritime strategy peculiarly suited to the tasks the Navy would have to carry out in peace or war. Sherman had also become his service's spokesman on unification. He focused on missions that the Navy could perform best and tied his positions on unification to the Navy's control of the resources necessary to pursue its strategy. The Navy's strategy and its policy towards unification were inextricably mixed in Sherman's mind, in the Navy's plans, and in the compromises reached during negotiations with the Army.

In Sherman's absence, Admiral Arthur W. Radford, Vice Chief of Naval Operations, dominated the OPNAV bureaucracy. Radford's views on national strategy, unification, an independent air force, service roles and missions, and the function of naval aviation differed from Sherman's. Many of Radford's positions were considered and rejected during 1946 and 1947, not only by the other services but also by the Navy's senior civilian and military leaders—Secretary Forrestal and Admiral Nimitz.

Forrestal first turned to Radford to serve as the spokesman for the Navy in the unification negotiations. As head of what was known at first as the Radford Committee, and later the Secretary's Committee on Research on Reorganization (SCOROR), Radford bore the onus of negotiating with Army representatives the draft of a unification plan acceptable to both services.

Central to the unification struggle was the role of aviation. Many

Midway moves through heavy seas off Sicily in February 1949.
(80-G-706984)

regarded Radford as the chief advocate of the naval aviation community—a "hard liner." His response to Basic Post War Plan No. 1, for
example, had recommended a virtual doubling of the number of carriers in the fleet, a politically unrealistic proposal.

By the fall of 1946, the burdens of the interservice struggle combined with other duties—he had replaced Mitscher as DCNO (Air)
in January 1946—led Radford to seek release from his unification
responsibilities. When, at a critical point in the negotiations, Secretary Forrestal asked Radford to work with Major General Lauris
Norstad on a compromise unification plan, Radford suggested that
Sherman assume the responsibility. Radford later credited his successor and Norstad with ultimately "removing the impasse between
the services."[2]

Radford expressed relief when he was assigned command of the
Second Task Fleet following Mitscher's death on 3 February 1947.[3]
The orders meant "leaving Washington just as the battle over unifica-

tion moved to Congress," Radford wrote, and he "could not help but feel that both personally and officially this was for the best." Radford was well aware that Forrestal had come to consider him too "hard line." Nimitz, too, had grown disgruntled with his deputy.[4]

Even before Radford's transfer to Second Fleet, Sherman, whose primary responsibility was strategic planning, had become Nimitz's spokesman in the unification negotiations.[5] The Nimitz-Sherman relationship was well established. Sherman had been Nimitz's chief planner in the Pacific from late 1943 until the end of the Pacific war. "'Ask Forrest,'" Clark Reynolds wrote, "was a byword of the Pacific Fleet staff at Pearl Harbor from late November 1943 until the Japanese surrender in August 1945."[6] Nimitz asked Sherman to stand behind him at the Japanese surrender ceremony on board *Missouri*.[7] As the Deputy CNO responsible for plans, Sherman operated as he had during the war, and Nimitz continued to rely upon him.

While Sherman and Radford were aviators, they disagreed over naval aviation's place in a more unified defense establishment. Sherman was more amenable to compromise and supported the development of a balanced fleet and the establishment of an independent air

Philippine Sea departs Grand Harbor, Malta, on 21 February 1949. (80-G-402225)

Vice Admiral Arthur W. Radford, Vice Chief of Naval Operations, July 1948. (80-G-705757)

force. Sherman was a centrist, not a partisan aviator. He defended battleships before Congress late in the war; not as the Navy's primary capital ship, but as a complement to the fleet's fighting strength. Sherman saw the need for a proper mix of forces—carrier and land-based air, surface, amphibious, and submarine. That Forrestal and Nimitz eventually turned to Sherman to work out unification problems with the Army came as no surprise. By 1947 "Ask Forrest" once again became a byword at Nimitz's headquarters.[8]

Like Radford, Sherman was eager to escape "the battle of Washington." After almost five straight years of staff duty, it was imperative that he receive a major seagoing command.[9] On his return from Europe in mid-1946, Sherman lobbied Nimitz to send him to the Mediterranean. By 1947 his involvement in the unification struggle made him more eager to avoid the maelstrom.

But as Sherman became the Navy's preeminent voice on unification and strategy, the balance of power within the Navy began to shift. By late 1947 Forrestal had left the Navy Department to become the nation's first Secretary of Defense. Nimitz, whom Sherman had served for so long, had announced his intention to retire.

At the end of 1947 the unification debate intensified. Those who thought that the Sherman-Norstad effort had marked the end of the

Forrestal and Radford converse in Washington on 6 May 1946.
(80-G-701914)

interservice struggle found themselves once again fending off Army
and Air Force attacks. Debate within the Navy increased as well.

With the Navy's position on strategy and unification in transition,
the appointment of Nimitz's successor as CNO took on added importance. The conservative "Gun Club" supported Blandy, a surface officer who had managed the Navy's nuclear tests in the Pacific. Forrestal,
Nimitz, and Sherman, all of whom favored a compromise on unification and accepted the establishment of a separate air force, supported
a centrist and aviator, Admiral DeWitt Clinton Ramsey, Vice Chief
of Naval Operations. But the aviation community supported a non-
aviator—Louis Denfeld. An emissary from aviator "Jocko" Clark had
met secretly with Denfeld at his CINCPACFLT headquarters in Hawaii and had struck a deal: for the aviators' support, Denfeld promised to name Radford as vice chief.[10]

Following Denfeld's selection, Sherman could have had little doubt that Radford would dominate OPNAV and make the aviators' extreme position the Navy's. Sherman, about to depart Washington for the relative safety of the Mediterranean, took the defeat philosophically, remarking to Ramsey, *"L'homme propose Le Dieu dispose!"* [11] He wrote Denfeld:

> It is obvious that the months ahead are going to be difficult ones in many ways—particularly in Washington—and I hope that even from a distance I can help to keep the people convinced of their need for a Navy. If there is ever anything I can do—with visiting dignitaries, or with the press at home or abroad—or in any other way, no inconvenience will ever stand in the way.
>
> Actually I feel that you and Raddy are unquestionably the best team to handle the battle of Washington and I know that the service as a whole shares that feeling. [12]

♦   ♦   ♦

Nimitz, Forrestal, and Sherman on board CINCPAC's barge in Guam, 1945. (NH 62530)

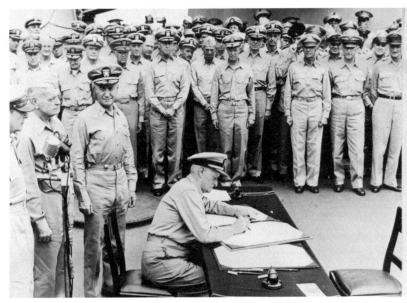

The Japanese surrender ceremony, 2 September 1945, on board the *Missouri* in Tokyo harbor. Rear Admiral Sherman stands with Admiral William F. Halsey (*left*) and General of the Army Douglas MacArthur behind Fleet Admiral Nimitz. (80-G-701293)

Nimitz rides triumphantly through Washington in October 1945 with Sherman at his right hand. (NH 58261)

Denfeld's and Radford's return to OPNAV as CNO and VCNO, respectively, came at a time of troubles for the Navy. The renewed unification debate intensified, the pressures exacerbated by the prospect of shrinking budgets. As the crisis deepened during 1949, the very survival of the Navy as anything more than a transport service was at stake. To weather these difficult straits, the Navy needed strong leadership and clear direction. It got neither.

Contemporaries generally portray Denfeld as an excellent officer of high moral integrity and, to some extent, a martyr for his cause. He was not an inspired leader. Admiral Charles D. Griffin, who worked for Sherman and Denfeld, remarked: "Admiral Denfeld is a very fine man. He would be the first to admit that he was not one of the most brilliant CNOs we ever had. He was no Forrest Sherman." [13] Vice Admiral Ruthven E. Libby believed that Denfeld made a grievous mistake by not resigning with Secretary of the Navy John Sullivan after the cancellation of the carrier *United States*. [14]

One of Denfeld's particular weaknesses was perhaps the most significant: he disliked his joint responsibilities—the ongoing unification struggle and service on the JCS. [15] Such duties fell to Radford and Vice Admiral Robert B. Carney, DCNO (Logistics) (OP-04), who stood "watch and watch." The latter added:

> Not only that but we also were doing all the work on the JCS, one or the other of us. Questions would come up on technical operations, where Raddy and I had lived through it and knew what the hell we were talking about . . . and Louie, he wouldn't know his ass from third base about it. [16]

Carney believed that Denfeld, who unlike his fellow chiefs had little wartime operational experience, was "helpless" in their company.

While Denfeld may have been a weak CNO, Radford, unlike his predecessor Ramsey, was a strong VCNO. Denfeld and Radford were both former DCNOs. They recognized that under Nimitz, comfortable with competent and eager subordinates, the Deputy Chiefs of Naval Operations had assumed an unintended prominence at the expense of VCNO Ramsey, on paper the principal advisor to the CNO and the coordinator of the work of the DCNOs. [17]

The revised 1948 OPNAV organizational manual reflected the VCNO's increased authority. [18] The vice chief's role as coordinator of the work of the deputy chiefs was reiterated and strengthened, with

Nimitz and Sherman
in Washington,
March 1947.
(NH 62452)

Secretary of the Navy
John L. Sullivan con-
gratulates Admiral
Louis E. Denfeld, the
new CNO, on 15 De-
cember 1947.
(80-G-704743)

the instruction that "all orders issued by the Vice Chief of Naval Operations in performing duties assigned him are considered as emanating from the Chief of Naval Operations and have the full force and effect as such."[19]

(As VCNO, Radford became the new spokesman for the Navy on strategic and unification questions.[20] Radford, not Vice Admiral Arthur D. Struble, Sherman's replacement as DCNO (Operations), made the major strategic presentations before Congress.)

While many of Radford's strategic ideas were similar to Sherman's, their approach, development, and content differed significantly. Sherman had been first a strategist and only later a direct participant in the Army-Navy negotiations. He brought to the bargaining sessions with Norstad a well-developed strategic concept upon which he based his positions on unification. Radford, whose focus during 1946 and 1947 had been naval aviation and the interservice struggle, attempted to graft many of his views onto the Navy's existing strategic concept.

Several early drafts of "The Role of the Navy in the Future," a paper prepared under Radford's direction, called for carriers, employing the mobility and the surprise they had evidenced in the Pacific war, to strike at Soviet targets ashore. "In a war against Russia," according to one draft, "some of the areas from which mobile air power strikes could be launched include, among others, the North Sea, the Norwegian Sea, the Barents Sea, the Mediterranean, the Arabian Sea, and the Sea of Japan."[21] Under Sherman's direction, NSPS 3 had clearly stated that such strikes would be limited to targets related to the prosecution of the naval campaign. While the imprint of the 1946 and 1947 planning is evident in Radford's presentation, the nature of the targets and the purpose of the strikes—whether strategic or direct support for naval operations—went unstated. Another draft recommended the "projection of naval air power from our floating bases against hostile war-making potential" and the participation of naval air forces "in the detection and interception of hostile air power striking at our own vital sources of war potential."[22] These missions departed from NSPS 3 and challenged the mission of the developing strategic air force. Appearing before Congress in February, Denfeld, Radford, and Captain George W. Anderson focused not on strikes against Soviet air and submarine bases but on strategic roles.[23]

In a presentation delivered in the fall of 1948, Radford outlined missions that were clearly strategic in nature, that is, not directly related to the conduct of naval operations. "Naval air power," Radford stated, "is essential to meet known enemy capabilities of today and tomorrow. Its mobile carriers attack the points of origin of enemy long range bombers." He reiterated the more traditional missions as well: "those same aircraft can strike enemy submarine pens, building yards, and operating bases."[24]

(While the primary mission of naval aviation under Denfeld and Radford remained operations in direct support of a naval war, a desire for a wider role in a strategic bombing campaign is evident in presentations delivered during 1948.) Captain Lyman Thackrey in a paper prepared for Radford recommended that the Navy accept Air Force General Hoyt S. Vandenberg's statement that he was willing to consult the other services on their contributions to the strategic air campaign. Thackrey suggested that the Navy offer to place liaison officers on the Air Force's strategic planning staff.[25] He wrote:

> At the present time we have no representatives who work in close contact with the Air Force strategic planners. General Vandenberg's statement opens the door wide and gives the Navy a chance to place representatives in a position where they can observe to what extent the Newport agreement is being carried out. Such officers could protect the Navy's interests at the grass-roots level, before plans achieved a complete form which might be difficult to contest in a meeting of the Joint Chiefs of Staff. Furthermore, these liaison officers, through immediate acquaintance with Air Force planners could provide us with an intelligence source at present unavailable to us. . . .
>
> Although the Air Force would probably want to place liaison officers in our plans division, we could place them in A/SW planning where their sources of information would not be so broad as our comparative ones.
>
> A proposal to so place liaison officers would apply a test to the sincerity of the Air Force with respect to accepting naval cooperation in Strategic Air warfare.[26]

Discussion by senior OPNAV officials about naval participation in strategic missions represented more than mere ambiguity of purpose. In the spring of 1948 budget growth, not fiscal retrenchment, seemed the order of the day. The Czechoslovakian coup and the Berlin blockade galvanized congressional willingness to spend more on defense.

That mood was not, unfortunately, matched in the White House. Nevertheless, 1948 saw the services scrambling for their share of a larger defense pie, the first since the end of the war. Radford's statements regarding possible strategic uses of naval air power represented an intent to cash in on the new congressional disposition on defense spending and on the growing aviation mania that had seized the nation—heretofore primarily to the benefit of the Air Force)

While Secretary of Defense Forrestal struggled within the administration and with Congress to ensure that any funding strengthened a "balanced military establishment" for the United States, the Navy planned increases that predominantly benefitted aviation.[27]

Throughout 1948 OPNAV prepared its Basic Naval Establishment Plan for 1949. Completed in August, BNEP 1-49 called for minor force reductions over BNEP 1-48: from 767 ships to 731, from 278 major combatants to 270, from 4 battleships to 2, and from 146 de-

The Newport Conference at the Naval War College in August 1948. *Left to right:* Lieutenant General Lauris Norstad, General Hoyt S. Vandenberg, Lieutenant General Albert Wedemeyer, General Omar N. Bradley, Secretary of Defense James V. Forrestal, Admiral Louis E. Denfeld, Vice Admiral Arthur W. Radford, and Major General Alfred M. Gruenther. (80-G-400609)

stroyers and destroyer escorts to 135. The number of carriers, heavy and light, and cruisers was maintained at 11, 8, and 9, respectively. Light antiaircraft cruisers were actually increased by one, from 20 to 21. Readiness improved as well. Major combatants would be allowed 224 hours of underway operations, up from 180 in BNEP 1-48.

The expansion of naval aviation was marked, from a force of 2,506 combat aircraft to one of 3,467, an increase of 38 percent, almost entirely in the attack carrier component.[28] BNEP 1-49 increased the Navy's carrier attack groups from 13 to 24, from 1,281 aircraft to 2,064, an increase of 61 percent.[29] During 1948 Radford guided the implementation of OP-05's "Full Air Program" that envisioned a 14,500-plane naval air force. The plan recommended the maintenance of 24 active and 8 reserve air groups to support a force struc-

Air Force B-36 bombers overfly the Capitol on Inauguration Day, 20 January 1949. (K-5130 U.S. Air Force)

A Navy P2V Neptune makes a jet assisted takeoff (JATO) from *Franklin D. Roosevelt,* 26 September 1949. (80-G-419106)

ture with 12 active and 4 inactive carriers.[30] Radford's replacement as DCNO (Air), Vice Admiral John Dale Price, was willing to see further decreases in the Navy's ship strength to attain that end.[31] The lessons of the Pacific war had demonstrated that only the readiness of 1.5 air groups for each heavy carrier would allow the Navy to conduct sustained operations.

In proposing the "Full Air Program," men like Price and Radford offered more than a partisan plan for naval aviation. They identified weaknesses inherent in a system in which fully operable carriers could be left standing about for want of fresh air groups. Such a fate had befallen the Japanese during the 1941–1945 war. The U.S. Air Force, Admiral Price pointed out to General Carl Spaatz, maintained a similar system to replace worn and tired squadrons. And Radford, Price, and others recognized that Congress, willing to fund aviation expansion in the Navy and Air Force, was not necessarily prepared to support a larger surface Navy. Price warned Denfeld that if the Navy did not propose to spend its additional money on aircraft, those funds would be shifted to the Air Force.[32]

Thus, Radford's remarks about the possible strategic tasks for naval aviation must be seen within the context of the Navy's growing competition with the Air Force for more budget dollars. To justify a larger air arm, Radford broadened the range of aircraft missions. NSPS 3 had, after all, raised the prospect that naval aircraft would aid the strategic air force by suppressing Soviet fighter opposition. Radford elaborated and expanded on that role. It would have been foolish to rule out such cooperation. Was not the ultimate aim of unification more effective interservice cooperation?

Under Nimitz and Sherman in 1946 and 1947, the Navy had begun to develop the capability to take part, if so directed, in operations beyond the immediate conduct of a naval campaign. Under Denfeld and Radford, the Navy demanded a larger role in the prosecution of strategic air warfare. Internally, the Navy's air arm dominated OPNAV, as was to be expected after the victory in the Second World War. And many surface and submarine officers identified the Navy's expansion policy as the program of the aviators, not of the Navy as a whole. Tensions increased within the Navy. But if naval aviation stood to gain the most in the short-lived expansion of 1948, it had the most to lose when the budget axe fell the following year.

And Radford's strategic concept, as presented to Congress, contained an inherent paradox. He rejected the Air Force's argument that it could "win a Russian war quickly and completely by the application of a single military force—long range bombing by atomic weapons." Yet at the same time, he argued that the Navy could perform that strategic role as well as, if not better than, the Air Force. Radford contended that carrier-based aircraft could prevent Soviet strategic bombing of the United States. Air defense, Radford stated, was essential because a Soviet air offensive could destroy the economic power of the country. Captain Thackrey noted the inconsistency: why would a Soviet strategic bombing campaign succeed when a U.S. Air Force operation would not?[33] Why argue for a Navy role in a mission that Radford expected would not yield the promised results?[34]

◆　◆　◆

The budget cuts of early 1949 threw the entire American defense establishment into chaos as force contraction displaced hope for expansion. Firm leadership became a dire necessity with fiscal retrenchment and a heightened unification struggle, exacerbated by, but by no means solely attributable to, the positions adopted by Radford and other Navy leaders.

The interservice debate over funding, roles, and missions focused on the Air Force's B-36 intercontinental bomber and the Navy's planned supercarrier—the *United States* (CVA-58). The Navy had sound reasons to construct a new class of aircraft carriers, unrelated to its potential use as a strategic platform, conventional or atomic. The need for a larger carrier had been recognized before the end of the Second World War. A supercarrier would permit more sustained employment overseas; would provide a larger, heavier, and therefore superior platform for Arctic operations; and would allow the operation of more and larger aircraft, including the AJ-1 Savage, an atomic strike bomber. Planning for the carrier and the naval bomber had begun during Nimitz's tenure as CNO.[35]

But during 1948, many in the Congress and the public began to perceive the *United States* primarily as an atomic platform and the Navy's strategic counterpart to the B-36. To *Chicago Tribune* reporter Lloyd Norman, the Denfeld-Radford portrayal of the Navy and its supercarrier as competitors to the Air Force and its B-36 was destined to fail. Corresponding with Sherman in the Mediterranean, Norman warned that the approach would backfire, for the new service and its bomber had captured the public's mind.[36] A week later Secretary of Defense Louis Johnson reversed Forrestal's decision to construct the *United States*.

The cancellation of the Navy's first postwar carrier marked the nadir of the Denfeld-Radford administration. Lloyd Norman observed that Denfeld's reliance on congressional friends and his wooing of Republican politicians were tactical mistakes. The Chicago columnist saw a need for a change in the Navy's leadership. "I am sure that you will soon be back here," Norman wrote Sherman, "you are needed desperately. Even men close to Denfeld say that you should take Radford's place."[37]

Indeed, Radford, VCNO for only sixteen months, was relieved and ordered to Hawaii on 30 April as CINCPAC/CINCPACFLT.[38] Denfeld turned to Vice Admiral Price, whom Radford considered his "alter ego in handling interservice air matters" and his chosen successor.[39]

But Denfeld, not Radford in Hawaii nor Price in Washington, now dominated OPNAV. Throughout 1949 the CNO wielded the budget axe, an axe that fell most heavily on naval aviation and Radford's Pacific command. Completed less than a week after Denfeld's firing, BNEP 1-50 pared another 43 ships from the Navy's rolls, from 731 to 688, although the number of major combatants actually rose for the first time since the end of the war, from 270 to 279. Major reductions by type included: carriers, 11 to 8; battleships, 2 to 1; and antiaircraft cruisers, 21 to 8. The number of several classes increased: heavy cruisers, 9 to 10; destroyers, 135 to 155; and light carriers, 8 to 11. The carrier air groups suffered draconian cuts: from 36 groups and 2,567 planes to 14 groups and 1,522 planes, a decrease of 40 percent.[40] Together, the reduction of the larger carriers, entirely at the expense of Radford's Pacific Fleet, and the severe cuts to naval aviation struck at the heart of the U.S. Navy's offensive capability.

To see the Navy through such a difficult period, the service needed a forceful CNO on the JCS and a strong administrator in OPNAV. Admiral Denfeld was the wrong man, in the wrong place, at the wrong time. As the pressures on the Navy increased throughout 1949 and further budget cuts and force reductions were outlined by the administration and the JCS, the Navy's internal discipline collapsed. When Radford was VCNO, the Navy at least had an ardent, if over-zealous, advocate who provided a clear sense of direction.

As the crisis deepened, Radford once again played a major role in the "battle of Washington." In the fall of 1949 Radford and his supporters, especially his old SCOROR staff, now OP-23 under Captain Arleigh Burke, prepared for a direct confrontation with the Air Force before Congress—the B-36 hearings. At stake was the Navy's survival as something more than a mere transport service. Jeopardized as well was the security of the nation, for these officers sincerely believed that the Air Force's strategic concept, in the words of Air Force officer and historian Harry Borowski, posed a "hollow threat."[41] Radford and scores of other naval officers were prepared to, and did, risk their careers during the hearings "to stand up and be counted," as Admiral Carney viewed it. Others termed the affair the "Revolt of the Admirals."

Although some doubted the wisdom of Radford's tactics, most naval officers believed that such a stand was necessary. Admiral Conolly, CINCNELM, whom many senior naval officers expected to succeed Denfeld, returned to Washington with Sherman for the hearings.[42] Conolly first conferred with Denfeld and Radford. He later described his reaction: "Denfeld was completely under the control of Radford, who was vice-chief, and he supported Radford in all of his contentions." He added: "Now, I have been told that Radford stated the case for the Navy. This thing wasn't as simple as that. Actually, what Radford was stating was the case for naval aviation."[43] After sitting through a trial run of the Navy's presentation for the hearings, Conolly termed the proceedings an "animal act." The traditional mode of testifying had long been established and remains so. The Secretary of the Navy leads off with his testimony, followed in order by the CNO and lower ranking admirals from OPNAV and the operating forces. Radford inverted the order and, Conolly believed, placed "the cart before the horse." Radford's assurances that the plan for the overall scheme had been worked out with the advice of public relations "experts" left Conolly feeling no more confidant.[44] He took his reservations to Denfeld, who seemed to share Conolly's doubts and promised to confer with Radford. But in the end Denfeld stood with Radford and the other senior officers.[45]

From Radford's perspective, a traditional approach to the hearings was out of the question. Secretary of the Navy Francis P. Matthews supported Secretary of Defense Johnson, not the Navy. Denfeld tarried undecided as to what stand he would take until the day before the hearings began. The support of few Navy senior horses gave Radford little choice but to lead with the cart.

During the congressional hearings on the B-36 bomber, held between 7 and 17 October 1949, Admiral Radford launched a direct attack on Air Force concepts of strategy, unification, tactics, and the capabilities of weapon systems, including the B-36.[46] To the surprise of many, Denfeld followed suit. He criticized the Air Force for its attempt to monopolize strategic forces, questioned the operational capability of the B-36, and faulted unification in principle and practice.[47]

The B-36 hearings ended Denfeld's career. On 27 October 1949— Navy Day—and less than a fortnight after the hearings, Secretary Johnson relieved the CNO of his duties.

Although Radford completed a long and distinguished career, serving as the Chairman of the Joint Chiefs of Staff under President Dwight D. Eisenhower from 1953 to 1957, for the short term his star fell as well.[48]

Vice Admiral Sherman rode out the tempest in the wardroom of his Sixth Task Fleet flagship in the Mediterranean, but openly discussed his decision to remain silent and to maintain a low profile.[49] Denfeld and Radford had asked Sherman to prepare a statement for the hearings. In his prepared testimony, Sherman wrote of a "balanced fleet" and the broad capabilities of aircraft carriers and surface ships. He also addressed the need for "balance" in the national military establishment.

Admiral Richard L.
Conolly,
CINCNELM,
London, February
1950. (NH 85176)

Nimitz and Sherman in New York City on 7 December 1949.
(NH 62374)

Secretary of the
Navy Francis P.
Matthews
(NH 77355)

In making a plea for adequate ready naval forces it is not intended that they be maintained at a level which will throw the military establishment out of balance. Balance must be maintained. We
need long range air force elements ready for action preferably in
forward positions such as the bomber groups now in England, and
if the B-36 is not a good bomber the Air Force should get a better
one. The need for maintaining a Navy does not depend on the
merits or defects of any particular bomber.[50]

Not surprisingly, Radford rejected Sherman's statement, considering
it "wishy-washy" and "compromising."[51] Sherman was sent back to
the Mediterranean. Before his departure, he confided to Mrs. Conolly
that he believed that her husband would most likely replace Denfeld
as CNO.[52]

Sherman's decision worked to his advantage. When the administration began to search for Denfeld's replacement, Sherman was
one of a few senior officers not "tar brushed" by the B-36 hearings.[53]
On 31 October 1949 Truman offered to return Nimitz to duty as
CNO; Nimitz refused. Asked for a recommendation, Nimitz suggested Sherman or Conolly. "And of the two, which would you rec-
ommend?" Truman asked. "Sherman is younger," Nimitz replied,
"and even less involved in politics."[54]

5 · A Strategy Reasserted

As Truman and Nimitz conferred, Sherman prepared his return to Washington. American officials drove down from Damascus and contacted the Sixth Task Fleet commander, then in Beirut. Secretaries Johnson and Matthews had settled on Sherman as their choice for CNO and, using State rather than Navy Department communications, instructed him to return to the United States in civilian clothes via a commercial airliner.[1] Sherman's absence from the recent hearings, his role in the unification negotiations during 1946 and 1947, and his youth made him the logical candidate.[2] Carney recalled:

> Forrest was the logical person to come in, and Raddy and I, we both knew that Forrest had always tried to put the banana peel under both of us anytime he could, because he considered, there's no two ways about it, that we were rivals and he wasn't about to give us a head start. But we both thought that he was the logical one to go in there, and Raddy and I laughed about it, we said we couldn't have a chance of a snowball in hell of even getting in, and if we did we couldn't have been effective.[3]

A series of delays punctuated Sherman's return flight. A concerned vice president of Pan American World Airways, Jack Towers, under whom Sherman had served in the Pacific, monitored the passage.[4] But Sherman considered the stops to his advantage and used them to glean information from newspapers and reporters as he neared home. Despite his "secret" return, the press speculated openly about his approach.[5] Sherman conferred with Matthews on 1 November and was sworn in the following day, pending the approval of the Senate.

Admiral Sherman was well known to the naval officer corps and his ambitions were no secret.[6] Admiral Carney related that "during the war and shortly after its conclusion, people were very wary about Forrest. They knew he was smarter than hell; they knew he had ambitions; they knew he was going to push them the best way he could."[7] Still, Sherman's appointment surprised many, not least Sherman himself. He expected Conolly to be the next CNO. At the most, he had hoped to replace Conolly as CINCNELM.[8] Shortly after his appointment, Sherman wrote Towers:

> As you know, I have always set my sights high, but had no wish to be assigned to duty in Washington at this time. The develop-ments which preceded my assignment were not to my liking and the assignment at this time was not of my seeking. However, under the circumstances, I consider it my duty to turn to and do the best job that I can.[9]

Barely fifty-three years old, Sherman was conscious of his junior status throughout his tenure. He had jumped ahead of many senior officers. One day Admiral Conolly was his superior and the next, his subordinate. Thus, Sherman, somewhat isolated as CNO, was under extreme pressure to prove himself and ultimately worked himself to death.[10]

Many men who worked with or for Sherman were duly impressed by his brilliance. Eisenhower thought he possessed "a sensitive and logical concern for the national picture, as opposed to any more nar-row one."[11] Army Major General Alfred M. Gruenther considered Sherman at the time of his appointment "probably the smartest U.S. planner living today."[12] General of the Army Omar N. Bradley judged him a gifted and outstanding strategist and later wrote: "The choice of CNO to replace Denfeld was a fortunate one—Forrest P. Sherman, one of the most impressive military officers I ever met . . . urbane, intellectual, diplomatic and smart as a whip."[13] This was a compli-ment from Bradley, who during the B-36 hearings called the Navy's admirals "Fancy Dans." For if any admiral was perceived as a "Fancy Dan," it was Forrest Sherman, who reportedly dined formally with his wife each evening.[14]

Sherman was an intellectual in uniform. Between 1926 and 1934

Secretary of Defense
Louis Johnson and
CNO Sherman ob-
serve maneuvers in
March 1950.
(SC 338221 U.S. Army)

he contributed frequently to the *Proceedings*. His articles, commen-
taries, and book reviews demonstrated an advanced grasp of history.
He wrote an extensive comment on the naval aspects of the Vicks-
burg campaign of the American Civil War, one article on Britain's use
of Guantanamo, Cuba, as a base in the eighteenth century, and another on air operations in Palestine during the Great War. He reviewed three volumes of the papers of Admiral Byng as they were
published by the Navy Records Society in Great Britain.[15]

In a January 1926 article entitled "Air Warfare," Sherman disagreed with Army aviators who demanded the creation of a separate
air force. He saw no need for an independent air force until the
United States possessed bases within range of a potential adversary's
homeland, or until an enemy had bases within range of the United
States. With the likely expansion of the number of services, Sherman
foresaw increased difficulty in the conduct of joint operations.

The only possible solution of the problem lies in forming a joint war staff for controlling the operations of all the armed forces of a country in such a manner that they will afford each other mutual support and function as integral parts of the country's united offensive power.[16]

Sherman also recognized the importance of offensive air warfare. In "Air Tactics and Strategy," which appeared in May 1926, he stated: "It was proven many times during the World War that the principle of the offensive was most important in air warfare, that the best defense against aircraft is to attack the enemy air force from the air, destroy his planes, his hangers, and his supply bases."[17]

In a June 1932 critical review of Admiral Sir Herbert Richmond's *Economy and Naval Security,* Sherman demonstrated his understanding of the revolution wrought in sea power by the aircraft carrier.

> With respect to aircraft carriers the author [Richmond] takes an attitude somewhat similar to that of the sailing-ship officers who deplored the advent of steam. He doubts the necessity for taking aircraft to sea and holds that "if both powers possess these vessels, neither is at an advantage over the other, and if neither has them, neither is at a disadvantage." He ignores the fact that fighting aircraft are an accepted part of the armament of nations and the fact that fleets must be able to operate within aircraft radius of enemy coasts, where if neither power has ship-based aircraft the enemy shore-based aircraft may dominate the situation. He ignores the ability of ship-based aircraft to operate against shore objectives with a degree of success which ships' guns could not possibly match.[18]

One can find in Sherman's early writings the origins of the strategic concept he laid before his OP-30 planners in June 1946, the positions he adopted regarding the establishment and role of the Air Force, and the compromise on defense unification he helped to forge. His knowledge of naval history and his experience as a naval aviator led Sherman to reject the argument that seaborne air power was unimportant for a naval power such as Britain, facing a land power such as Germany. He believed that carriers allowed a greater extension of sea power ashore, and that the offensive was central to that mission. He anticipated the establishment of an independent air force principally to conduct a strategic air offensive. He expected that development to herald some form of unified defense organization.

Given the content of Sherman's writings during the interwar years, his decision to avoid the B-36 controversy should come as no surprise. He refused to attack the Air Force's strategic primacy, suggested that it get a good long-range bomber, and supported the establishment of the Department of Defense. He still foresaw, as he had as OP-03, a more conventional role for the Navy. In his testimony prepared for Congress, he questioned the wisdom of considering the "concept of intercontinental warfare" as the American *"primary"* military mission. "Our national policies," Sherman would have reminded Congress, "involve helping peoples not in the same continent with us, and we have encouraged them to become our allies. We cannot afford in good faith, nor is it in our interest, to base our military preparations on abandoning these peoples and relying on exchanging destructive air attacks." [19]

But for all of his strengths, including his ability to work successfully with his Army and Air Force counterparts, Sherman had problems with the admirals and subordinates who viewed him ambivalently. As a midshipman at Annapolis he was considered "too smart." The *Lucky Bag,* the student yearbook, concluded:

> Forrest Percival has been the object of ridicule in some quarters and an envied example in others. Hard working and conscientious in the extreme, he . . . is our most convincing argument for the theory that "Brains is King." . . . Above all, Sherman knows his job; when he is given a thing to do he finds out all there is to be found about it, and the job is well done. [20]

Thirty years later, Mitscher, who disliked Sherman, considered him "too damned brilliant." [21] Navy Captain Edward Everett Hazelett, Jr., who in retirement corresponded regularly with Eisenhower, warned that Sherman was "sarcastic, a bit of a snob, and hard to know"; a man who would not be able to "make a recalcitrant and conservative Navy *like* what he forced down its throat." [22] Conolly, the true victim of the B-36 affair, portrayed Sherman as a "compromiser and temporizer." [23] Burke considered Sherman "brilliant" but styled the new CNO as "a late-come aviator. He was a man who wasn't really a skilled flyer but still was an aviation spokesman, and that griped." [24]

Burke's comments reveal more about the perceptions held by many senior naval officers than they do the facts. Sherman graduated from the Naval Academy second of 199 in his class of 1918 and earned his wings in 1922; "Jocko" Clark, who graduated in the same

Sherman and Radford confer in San Diego, California, June 1950. (80-G-427790)

class, earned his in 1925. Who would have termed "Jocko" Clark a "late-come aviator"?[25]

Sherman's decision to prepare testimony for the B-36 hearings, which he must have known would be unwelcomed and rejected by Radford, made him an outsider. Others, whatever their personal views, testified out of service loyalty.[26] Sherman's silence elevated him to the top of the promotion ladder.

His ability to work with other services may have demonstrated a concern for the national picture, as Eisenhower had commented, but it also marked the new CNO a compromiser to many in his own service. One of Sherman's favorite expressions was "tomorrow's another day." He did not publicly express the same sense of doom that pervaded Navy circles in 1949. He would show that there was another day for the Navy and that conciliation and negotiation worked.

An early test of those skills came in January 1950. Admiral Radford, Sherman's "shipmate" and "longtime friend," greeted his appointment with "mixed" feelings. Radford was concerned that Sherman had accepted the job with preconditions. Radford in Hawaii and Sherman in Washington arranged to meet half-way at the Los Angeles Navy Ball on 21 January 1950. Sherman reassured Radford that the new CNO was his own man, intent on healing the Navy's wounds, avoiding recriminations, and presenting a united service front within the Defense Department. Radford offered his congratulations. He told the CNO that "he was about the only man who could handle the job at that time."[27] Not long after the meeting, Radford wrote Rear Admiral Richard E. Byrd: "I feel that he [Sherman] has and is doing a splendid job—one that could not be done by anyone else on the active list that I know of."[28]

◆ ◆ ◆

Sherman discovered on his return to Washington that the inter- and intra-service debates of 1948 and 1949 had weakened his strategic concept developed during 1946 and 1947. As Chief of Naval Operations, he immediately reasserted his strategic concept and once again gave the Navy firm direction.

That concept, in the naval tradition, was a guideline, not a blueprint. Operational commanders were responsible for detailed planning and were best suited to test the strategy during peacetime through staff analysis and fleet exercises.

During 1948 and 1949 both CINCNELM and CINCPACFLT undertook studies that recommended a cautious application of a forward, offensive strategy.[29] The CINCNELM study, completed late in 1948, concluded that an air defense phase might have to precede direct strikes against Soviet bases. At the outbreak of war, the Soviets would probably launch air strikes against American convoys and carrier task forces. The CINCNELM study envisioned initial operations resembling the World War II battle of the Philippine Sea; a "Turkey Shoot" in which the Soviets would dissipate their air power in futile attacks against American carrier task forces. The study concluded:

> Since it is not envisaged that the supply of fast carriers, carrier aircraft, and pilots will increase as rapidly as the demand, it is necessary to avoid bulling our way into a shore-based air "hornets nest" until such time as we are confident we can do so and come out the winner. This can only be determined by experience. *In other words, initially probe: determine reaction: and then operate accordingly.*[30]

The insertion of a preliminary defensive phase into the Navy's basic strategic concept ironically involved Sherman himself, for the study drew heavily on his experience as Commander Sixth Task Fleet. But the study retained as its ultimate objective direct strikes on Soviet air and naval bases, and recommended the preparation of Turkish airfields to accommodate naval attack aircraft for occasional surprise attacks on Black Sea complexes.[31]

A CINCPACFLT staff study, Brightness, introduced a similar note of circumspection.[32] The study envisioned forward, offensive operations at the outbreak of hostilities "against Soviet air, submarine, and other important bases in the *Kuriles,* southern *Kamchatka,* including *Petropavlovsk,* and southern *Sakhalin.*" Whereas Sherman in the June 1946 meeting with his OP-30 staff had estimated that the Navy's Pacific Fleet could quickly "wipe up" Soviet Far Eastern naval and air assets, Brightness was less optimistic. It suggested that Eastern Pacific task groups, earmarked to reinforce Europe (the swing strategy), steam by way of Japan, temporarily "assisting hard-pressed Far East Command forces by carrier strikes of several days duration." Judiciously executed surprise strikes, in and out operations, against Soviet bases would prevent a concentrated attack by land-based aircraft against a weak force of American carriers.

In June 1948 the General Board also introduced a note of caution into the Navy's strategic planning. "National Security and Navy Contributions Thereto for the Next Ten Years," written primarily by Captain Arleigh Burke, recognized the strategic value of direct strikes on Soviet air and submarine bases, but questioned the Navy's ability to carry them out.

> It is the duty of the Navy to maintain control of the seas. *Russia* can challenge our control of the seas with submarines and air power; both require bases. Early destruction of *Russia's* bases and denial of advanced bases to her will necessitate heavy attacks immediately in different areas. There will be so many demands made upon the Navy for immediate operations in widely separated parts of the world that fulfillment of all the demands may well be beyond the capacity of the *United States* Navy.[33]

The Navy's changed priorities also challenged Sherman's strategic concept. The effort to develop new ASW tactics and technology, accorded importance equal to the development of the nuclear program by Nimitz, received less support during 1948 and 1949. Denfeld and his deputy, Radford, shifted the emphasis from a balanced Navy to an aviation-oriented fleet. Congress, alarmed by the Navy's apparent declining interest in ASW, appropriated $20 million specifically for airborne antisubmarine development. But when Secretary of Defense Johnson ordered the Navy to slice $198 million from its budget, Admiral Denfeld included the $20 million appropriation in that cut, a decision poorly received on the Hill.[34]

(But the lessened attention to the Soviet submarine threat resulted in part from the Navy's initial overreaction to it in 1946 and 1947. The specter of hundreds of Soviet submarines surging into the Atlantic and Pacific at the outbreak of war, as Sherman briefed President Truman in January 1947, was inaccurate)

In August 1949, a study generated by the Air Warfare Division of DCNO (Air) on the development of carrier aviation concluded that the Soviet submarine threat had been exaggerated and could be "throttled" early in a war. Soviet air power posed the real threat to the Navy's use of the sea. The study rejected the cautious strategy advocated by the CINCNELM study and recommended the aggressive operations envisaged in the Navy's initial postwar plans.[35]

Studies generated by the Navy's intelligence and ASW communities also played down the immediate subsurface threat. Early in January 1949 the Assistant Chief of Naval Operations for Undersea Warfare, Rear Admiral Charles B. Momsen, directed a committee of the Submarine Conference to consider a Russian submarine offensive against the United States and the United Kingdom. The committee's report highlighted the general limitations on what the Soviets could do in the Atlantic with the submarines and bases available to them.[36]

A presentation on Soviet undersea warfare capabilities, prepared for a November 1949 conference on ASW, similarly concluded:

> As for capabilities and intentions, it may be stated rather tritely that Soviet submarines today present a threat which is serious but not overwhelming. In other words, they could cause considerable disruption and sink a large number of ships, but we do have the weapons and techniques to counter the threat of Soviet submarines today. In this connection, it is important to differentiate between Soviet capabilities and intentions. A full exploitation of the capabilities of Soviet submarines would give us a rather bad time. But so far as we can determine, their intentions are still limited by the defensive and land-bound concept.[37]

The "Study of Undersea Warfare," begun at the direction of Forrest Sherman a fortnight after he assumed his duties as CNO and completed on 22 April 1950, reached the same conclusion. The Soviets had neither built nor deployed a large submarine fleet, despite their possession of German technology and the necessary resources. Equipped with obsolescent U-boat types, without snorkels and other modern developments, the Russian submarine force posed a less serious threat than anticipated.[38]

Nevertheless, the shift in emphasis from the Soviet submarine to the air threat has been overdrawn by historians. While various studies correctly dismissed the immediate undersea Soviet threat, the ASW community was concerned for the future. For example, the April 1950 study also concluded that the "Anti-Submarine Warfare techniques and equipment in use by the U.S. Navy at the present time, while adequate to defeat the conventional World War II type submarines [the type the Russians were using] are inadequate to deal with an advanced-type of submarines and weapons that the Russians can build now."[39] Five years after the war the U.S. Navy still lacked the means to counter the German-designed Type XXI boat. Advances in propulsion and weaponry were expected as the United States and the Soviet Union developed nuclear-propelled submarines and guided missiles capable of carrying atomic warheads. If the Navy was to meet the potential Soviet threat, technological development could not be delayed.[40]

Others in OPNAV considered the Soviet air threat, not the submarine threat, exaggerated. An OPNAV presentation of 2 August 1950 to the Weapons Systems Evaluation Group, which was studying air defense of carrier task forces, concluded: "We do not claim that the Fleet Air Defense system is, or will be, impregnable. But we do claim a most effective, and a more concentrated air defense than almost any other Air Defense system."[41] The JCS initiated the study earlier in the year to examine the offensive and defensive capabilities of carrier task forces operating in the Mediterranean and Barents Seas during a hypothetical war in 1951. Sherman suspected that the JCS assumed the study would condemn the carrier task force as hopelessly obsolescent. But the study, completed early in 1952, after Sherman's death, supported the capabilities of the carrier task force and concluded that "unless the Soviets successfully employ atomic weapons in numbers against the carrier forces, air opposition in the operating areas considered in this study would probably not provide a threat of damage sufficient to prevent operations of a task force containing four or more carriers."[42] Thus, carrier task forces could be deployed in the Mediterranean and in the Barents Sea and carry out offensive operations against Soviet bases.[43]

Throughout Sherman's tenure, the Navy remained of two minds. Did Soviet submarines or aircraft pose the greater threat to naval operations? The design of the *Forrest Sherman*-class destroyer, intended to serve as an ASW and an antiair platform, incorporated this ambiguity.[44] Nevertheless, Sherman as CNO reestablished the prominence of the Navy's ASW community. He chose Vice Admiral Lynde D. McCormick, a submariner, as VCNO. A renewed spirit permeated the fourth annual ASW conference, a meeting a disappointed Sherman could not attend. Captain Charles E. Weakley, commander of the Surface Anti-Submarine Detachment, noted the "verbal expression of priority" and the "overpowering attendance list" of the 1949 conference, no doubt spurred by the expected presence of the new CNO.[45]

The development of the submarine as an ASW platform was central to the Navy's antisubmarine effort and an important element in the conduct of a forward, offensive strategy. As early as 1946, Sherman and others had emphasized the future role of the killer submarine—the SSK. During the Second World War American submarines conducted a classic *guerre de course* that, in combination with other naval and air operations, isolated the Japanese home islands from their sources of raw material.

Although the Soviet Union possessed a merchant marine of some size, she relied far less on such transportation than had Japan. Instead, the Navy intended to convert a significant portion of the American undersea arm into a force of SSKs that in wartime would conduct forward, offensive operations in Soviet waters—hunting Soviet submarines at the source. Other submarines would conduct more traditional missions—minelaying, reconnaissance, and lifeguarding.[46]

But as the opening speaker of a November 1949 submarine conference admitted, "submarine peacetime deployment is based primarily on anti submarine warfare training. Deployment on D-Day is not the controlling factor."[47] Such a peacetime mission was unlikely to raise the morale and self-esteem of submariners in the wake of what they rightly perceived as a tremendous, if "silent," victory.[48] No DCNO for submarines had been created after the war. Officers squabbled over reduced billets. Many senior officers, such as Vice Admiral Charles A. Lockwood, Jr., retired. Those submariners who advanced usually did so outside their branch, for example Vice Admiral

James Fife, Jr., who served as DCNO (Operations) during 1952 and 1953. Even McCormick's advancement as VCNO was deceptive, for he had last served in submarines in 1931 and spent the war as a surface force commander and a staff officer in the Pacific and in Washington.[49]

Between the initial conception of SSK operations in 1946 and Sherman's return to Washington three years later, development had been slow. Not until early 1949 had OPNAV considered SSK operations technically feasible. Under the codename Project Kayo, Submarine Division 11 in the Pacific and Submarine Development Group 2 in the Atlantic began "'to solve the problem of using submarines to detect and destroy enemy submarines.'"[50]

The Atlantic group, consisting of the heavily modified fleet submarines *Tusk, Cochino, Toro,* and *Corsair,* prepared in the spring of 1949 for a cruise to the Grand Banks and the southern coast of Iceland. But Commander Submarine Force, Atlantic, with State Department approval, ordered the group to conduct an Arctic cruise in the Barents Sea instead. The American submarines operated within twelve miles of the North Cape as far as longitude 30° east. Despite the accidental loss of *Cochino* on 25 August, the SSK program was firmly established.[51]

The creation of the attack submarine force as a major component of a forward, offensive American naval strategy was one of the most significant, lasting achievements of the Navy's postwar leaders. Nimitz initiated the effort. Denfeld authorized the installation of an atomic power plant in a submarine. Work on the first nuclear-powered submarine *Nautilus* began during Sherman's tenure as CNO.[52]

◆ ◆ ◆

Restoring a sense of mission to his own service was but one of many problems confronting Sherman as CNO. At the joint level Sherman discovered a more difficult challenge to his strategic concept.

The strategic planning system, much more sophisticated in 1950 than in the days of the Pincher studies three years before, focused on three basic series of plans. The JCS 1844 series, bearing codenames such as Crosspiece, Pinwheel, Shakedown, Offtackle, and Doublestar, considered a war fought with existing forces. Completed shortly after Sherman's return to Washington as CNO, JCS 1844/46 projected an early offensive against Soviet shipping, naval and air forces, bases, and installations; and the initiation of a blockade and mining.

So too did the JCS 2143 series of intermediate-range plans (Headstone, Reaper, Oakwood) for a war beginning in 1954.[53]

The nation's long-range plan for a war in 1957, JCS 1920/5, code-named Dropshot, followed the same approach. Although the plan never received final JCS approval, it represented the state of American strategic thinking. Dropshot advocated an early offensive against Soviet submarines and aircraft and their bases and supporting facilities. The American planners considered Soviet merchant shipping a target of little importance. Soviet surface naval forces were considered capable only of "harassing attacks."

> Offensive operations against the source of these threats are considered the most effective and least expensive means of neutralizing them. These operations would have as their primary objectives the destruction of enemy naval and merchant shipping, submarine assembly and repair facilities, naval bases, and the air defenses of such supporting facilities. . . . Included also would be offensive mining of sea approaches to enemy ports and bases, hunter-killer operations, anti-submarine submarine operations, and the destruction of enemy naval forces which get to sea.
>
> Operations against those targets constituting the source of Soviet naval strength would be conducted principally by fast carrier task forces, hunter-killer groups and submarines, assisted by land-based air. . . . The air elements of the forces generated by this course of action would participate in the air offensive in coordination with the allied air forces, when available from primary tasks.[54]

Several charts and maps accompanying Dropshot designated the areas of operation and the forces assigned. From carrier staging areas (little silhouettes of *Midway*-class carriers) in the Barents Sea, the eastern and central Mediterranean, the Persian Gulf, the Bering Sea, and off the northeastern and southern coasts of Japan, radii of action extended 770, 1,220, and 1,500 miles into the Soviet Union. The inclusion in Dropshot of carrier operations in the Barents and Bering Seas marked a departure from the Pincher studies. Sherman, who had resisted earlier efforts to have the Navy operate in the far north, now believed that the service was prepared to conduct Arctic operations, as had Denfeld.

Admiral Sherman's basic strategic concept survived his absence from Washington, but the Navy's role in the implementation of that strategy did not. The extent to which the service lost ground within the planning process is less evident in the long and intermediate-range plans than it is in the emergency plan. Dropshot, for example, envisioned a gigantic effort employing dozens of United States and allied aircraft carriers, scores of air wings, and hundreds of ground divisions in an offensive along the periphery of the Soviet Union. Dropshot was as much a force goal to be met by a wartime industrial mobilization of the non-Soviet world as it was a strategy.

But Offtackle (JCS 1844/46), the plan for war in 1949 or 1950, involved an existing, weak force structure. Scarcity breeds competition in strategic planning and the differing views of the services thus came to the fore. On his return to Washington in November 1949, Sherman found OPNAV wholly dissatisfied with the state of Offtackle.[55]

Between 1947 and 1949 the changing international and domestic situations transfigured the strategic environment. The United States aligned itself with a European coalition—NATO—a development of great strategic significance, but one that shifted the center of gravity of American concern in the Old World from the Mediterranean and the Middle East to northern Europe. In Asia, Chiang Kai-Shek's retreat from the mainland, fears for his tenure on Taiwan, a deteriorating situation in Indochina, and trouble brewing in the Korean peninsula boded ill. In the meantime, a budget-conscious Truman administration and the Congress steadily reduced the Navy's forces with cuts that fell disproportionately on the Pacific Fleet. A six-carrier Navy—one-carrier Pacific Fleet—loomed on the fiscal 1950 horizon. The United States and its Navy faced an increasingly threatening world with steadily decreasing military resources.

On 9 November 1949, one week after Sherman became CNO, Captain Charles W. Lord in the Strategic Plans Division outlined the Navy's problem with Offtackle. "The force tabs for U.S. naval forces," Lord remarked, "are not indicative of either naval thinking or naval capabilities." The Secretary of Defense had supported the Army and Air Force demands to decrease the number of carriers mobilized for Offtackle from sixteen to ten. Only eight carriers would become active during the first two years of the war. Marine divisions were reduced from six to four.

"Besides being unable to comprehend why we do not plan to use our full capabilities in a strategic war plan," Lord commented, "we consider the plan defective in another sense." Strategic plans, Lord insisted, ought to "be logical extensions of peacetime policy." If sup-

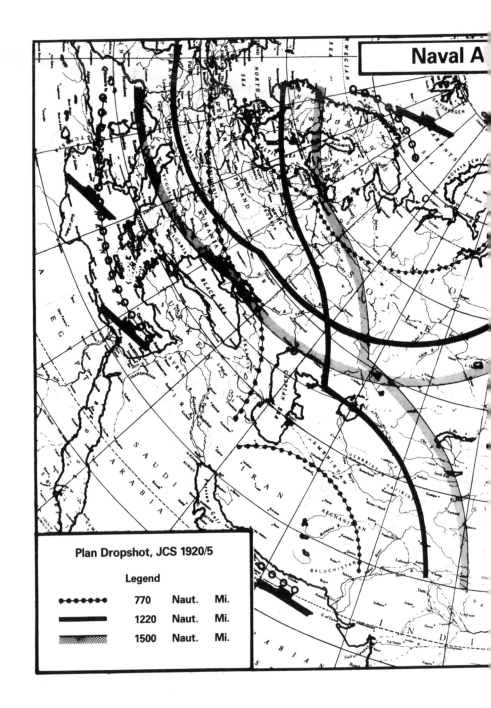

Naval A

Plan Dropshot, JCS 1920/5

Legend

••••••••	770	Naut. Mi.
▬▬▬▬	1220	Naut. Mi.
▨▨▨▨	1500	Naut. Mi.

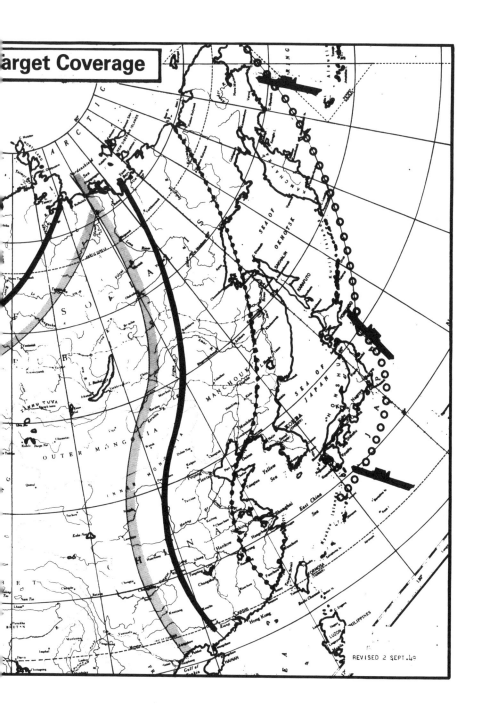

arget Coverage

REVISED 2 SEPT. 49

port for Great Britain was to be the centerpiece of American strategy, the oil-rich Middle East, a region the British considered vital to their security and the prosecution of a major war, was being ignored. The Truman Doctrine, worked out with Britain during 1946–1947, involved economic and military support for Greece and Turkey, nations that in all probability would be abandoned in an Offtackle war. Lord continued:

> The plan suffers, in our opinion, from a preoccupation with Western Europe as the only avenue leading to defeat of Soviet military forces. It lacks flexibility, in that no provision is made for alternate courses of action which might be preferable under certain circumstances. It inferentially places undue reliance on the results expected of the atomic phase of the strategic air offensive. And last, but not least, it provides for no diversionary action along the "soft underbelly" of Europe. From the aspect of the successful accomplishment of Task I (the security and utility of the U.K.) this is a serious and possible fatal defect, since the principal Soviet air effort both offensive and defensive can then be channeled against the U.K. and against the strategic bombing effort emanating from the U.K.[56]

In the struggle within the JCS over Offtackle during 1949 and 1950, one can see the origins of the strategic debate of the 1980s in which the merits of a continental or a maritime focus were argued. The Navy had its way by default during 1946 and 1947 in shaping a maritime strategy. At that time the Air Force was accorded the primary role in wartime of conducting the strategic air offensive. The Navy was assigned the secondary role of carrying out offensive operations to secure forward American bases and to attack those of the Soviets. The U.S. Army found itself reduced to a defensive mission. Its few divisions provided inadequate striking or defensive power to counter a massive Soviet ground attack.

But by 1949 the Army was recovering its strength and, under the leadership of Generals Eisenhower and Bradley, began to reassert itself in the nation's strategic planning process. NATO's potential to provide the ground divisions that would defend Western Europe further strengthened the Army's hand. The alliance commitment, not yet extended into the eastern Mediterranean, forced a revolution in postwar strategic planning that left the Mediterranean a secondary theater.[57]

Offtackle reflected strategic concepts familiar to Eisenhower and

Bradley, who had directed the American war effort in the European theater during the Second World War. Throughout that campaign Eisenhower had emphasized the primacy of the northwest European line of operations, a line extended from London, through Berlin, and now to Moscow. Eisenhower and Bradley viewed Mediterranean operations as they had during the past war, subsidiary actions best restricted to the western Mediterranean. Even here, the intention was not to operate in the Middle Sea per se, but to build up a base in northwest Africa for a return to a continent from which the allies would in all probability have been driven. (Offtackle was a planned replay of World War II operations Torch, Husky, Avalanche, Bolero, Roundup, Overlord, and Anvil-Dragoon.)

The U.S. Navy adopted Britain's World War II role, complete with Churchillian jargon. America's Navy planners understood the purpose of peripheral operations in dispersing enemy forces before a decisive campaign, much as Lord Alanbrooke, Britain's wartime Chief of the Imperial General Staff, viewed Mediterranean operations as secondary, but necessary preliminaries to a campaign in northwestern Europe. Furthermore, the need to force a dispersal of Soviet

General of the Army Douglas MacArthur with Army Chief of Staff General J. Lawton Collins and CNO Sherman in Tokyo on 21 August 1950. (80-G-422492)

Admiral Carney,
Commander in
Chief Allied
Forces, Southern
Europe, greets
CNO Sherman on
his arrival in Na-
ples, 20 July 1951.
(80-G-431945)

offensive efforts would be crucial in a third world war. Unlike the
Germans, the Soviets would have no second front tying down the
bulk of their army.

After Sherman reviewed Offtackle, he addressed the JCS for the
record, highlighting many of the deficiencies enumerated by Lord.
The CNO disliked the priority given to the defense of Great Britain
and Scandinavia at the expense of allied interests in the Mediterranean. He was also gravely concerned about the Pacific.

> There is likely to be need for deployment of a small carrier task
> force in the Pacific. As a matter of fact I am concerned over the
> current situation in the Pacific where the FY 1951 force level will be
> inadequate to cope with situations which may develop very soon.
> The security of Alaska and the Japan-Okinawa-Philippine line re-
> quires naval support.[58]

Only Sherman's timely personal intervention ensured that the Navy
had at least one carrier task force in the Western Pacific when the
North Korean army crossed the 38th Parallel.

◆ ◆ ◆

Admiral Sherman served as Chief of Naval Operations for twenty months. Although the outbreak of war in Korea in June 1950 and his untimely death in July 1951 limited his achievements, Sherman oversaw the Navy's renaissance.[59] He reiterated the basic strategic concepts he had first outlined in mid-1946.[60] Sherman stressed the central role of the carrier task force, the umbrella under which the Navy would carry out its many missions: antisubmarine warfare, amphibious operations, and air strikes against targets ashore. Questioned about Soviet bases during a February 1951 interview with *U.S. News and World Report,* he responded:

In that connection, the air-defense problem, and the anti-submarine problem have certain points of similarity. The worst place to protect a ship is where the ship is. The worst place to protect a convoy is at the convoy. The worst place to protect a city from air attack is at the city. The best place is at the bases from which the airplane or submarine comes. The next best place is en route—the worst place is at the target.[61]

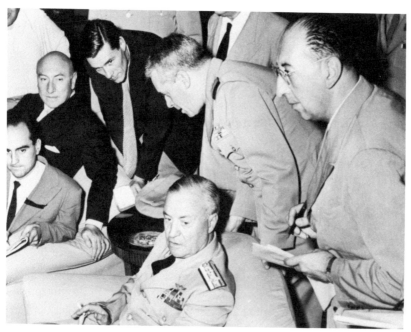

Sherman's final press conference, the Hotel Excelsior in Naples on 21 July 1951. (80-G-4319431)

Senior officers salute as Sherman's coffin arrives at National Airport in Washington on 25 July 1951. Front row (*left to right*): Generals Omar N. Bradley, Hoyt S. Vandenberg, and J. Lawton Collins; Admiral Lynde D. McCormick; Fleet Admiral Chester W. Nimitz; General Clifton B. Cates; and Admirals Thomas C. Kinkaid and William M. Fechteler. (80-G-431934)

To carry out that strategy, Sherman argued within the JCS and before Congress for an increase in naval forces, including a supercarrier, and a redirection of the nation's strategic focus.[62] At the time of his death, the Navy's carrier strength under the emergency war plan had been increased at D-day plus twelve months from eight to twelve, and the maximum number to be mobilized, from ten to sixteen. The four additional D+12 carriers were all to be employed in the Pacific. In the spring of 1950 Congress was in the mood to support a supercarrier for the Navy. By the fall, with a little help from the North Koreans, the Truman administration reconsidered and approved the construction of the *Forrestal* (CVA-59).[63] While Sherman proved unable to return the JCS's strategic orientation to the Mediterranean theater, he was able to place the allied command structure in that sea on a firm footing. He opened negotiations with the Spanish on base rights for the U.S. Navy, and emphasized the role of the Middle Sea in his own service's strategic thinking. Sherman was touring the Mediterranean when he died in Naples on 22 July 1951.[64]

Sherman restored harmony to the officer corps and balance to naval forces, missions, and priorities. While he reemphasized the roles of submarines and the ASW community, his most difficult and pressing task was restoring the morale and strength of naval aviation.[65] Under Sherman, the Navy's nuclear-powered program proceeded with renewed vigor. In Admiral Carney's words, Sherman proved himself "very strong; very confident."[66] His successor would inherit a service far different from that which had awaited Forrest Sherman on his return from the Mediterranean in late 1949. The Navy possessed a coherent strategic concept and a renewed faith in itself and its role in the American national security establishment.

6 • A Strategy Lost

THE Truman administration chose Admiral William M. Fechteler to succeed Sherman. Fechteler, a classic "old salt" officer, was senior to all but Radford and had avoided involvement in the "Revolt of the Admirals." Fechteler's forte was administration and he had made his mark, much as had Denfeld, in personnel. He had strong political ties, but limited wartime operational experience.[1]

That he inherited Sherman's established strategic concept was fortunate, for Fechteler lacked the intellectual gifts and driving force of his predecessor. His fellow chiefs considered him the weak link of the JCS.[2] The administration did not appoint Fechteler Chairman of the Joint Chiefs in 1953 even though a naval officer was due to succeed Bradley. Key officials believed he lacked the "prestige, war experience, strategic grasp," and personality to be chairman.[3] Nevertheless, Fechteler guided the expansion and modernization of the Navy when the services planned for, and argued over, the size of the post-Korean War defense establishment.

Rear Admiral Arleigh Burke was responsible for much of the Navy's success in the strategic arena during Fechteler's tour. As head of the Strategic Plans Division (OP-30), Burke oversaw the development of the Navy's Flotilla plan for carrier task forces and submarines to "operate offensively against enemy bases and areas and thus force the dispersion of his land and air strength" to the periphery.[4] In November 1952 Burke drafted Fechteler's response to a JCS review of the emergency war plan originated by the Supreme Allied Commander, Atlantic (SACLANT). Burke's approach identified Soviet vulnerabilities in a European war and emphasized how NATO's naval forces, including those in the United States, could exploit them. Burke restated a well-established theme.

> The enemy will have at his disposal submarines, aircraft, surface craft and other means which he can be expected to use singly and in combination in a manner which he believes will be most effective. The weapons which the enemy will use in his attempts to destroy our convoys and naval forces will be operated from shore bases. Consequently, the bases and facilities which directly support those weapons must also be destroyed or neutralized.[5]

In June 1952 testimony Fechteler outlined the Navy's strategic concept before Congress.

> What may not be understood is the fact that in the fast carrier task force the Navy has the ability to carry the war to the enemy in its initial stages, to knock out his coastal bases, to prevent him from receiving any outside help, and to put him on the defensive at the outset. I must add at this time that the fast carrier task force can do this if it is composed of modern ships, including large carriers capable of operating the newest and best planes.[6]

As potential Soviet threats to American control of the seas, Fechteler ranked submarines, first; shore-based aircraft, second; and the deployment of guided missiles, third. He ignored the Soviet surface fleet.

> Now, the most effective method of combating all three, is to get him where he lives. The least effective is at his target. The means whereby we go at him where he lives, that is, the submarine base, the shore air base, and the guided missile launching site, is with a fast carrier task force which reach in and get him [sic].

While the Navy's strategic concept was stated clearly and publicly, detailed discussions of possible naval operations in the North Atlantic and the Mediterranean were "off the record."

By the fall of 1952 Sherman's strategic concept had been well established at the combined, as well as the joint, national level. American, British, and Canadian (ABC) planning discussions had begun as early as 1946.[7] In October 1949 the North Atlantic Ocean Regional Planning Group (NAORPG), the precursor of NATO's SACLANT, met in Washington. One of five regional groups established during NATO's first council meeting in September 1949, NAORPG's opening session established five subgroups. Membership in the first group was limited to the alliance's principal naval powers, Britain and the United States. Initially designated "Offensive Operations and Attack at Source," the subgroup prepared "broad plans for offensive action against enemy armed forces and shipping, their bases and port facilities, including attack at source, amphibious and airborne operations, and offensive mining."[8]

British naval strategists shared many of the ideas of their American counterparts with regard to the prospects of a European war. For example, a 1951 report of the Sea Air Warfare Committee concluded:

> The war cannot be won by defensive action alone and therefore attacks against enemy submarine and air bases will be a major factor in achieving our aim of maintaining sea communications. Consideration of such offensive methods is outside the scope of this paper but the proportion of our total resources allotted to such offensive and defensive tasks may have a decisive effect on our whole maritime strategy.[9]

In April 1953 Field Marshall Viscount Montgomery of Alamein suggested to an audience at the National War College in Washington that NATO's first job was to hold the flanks by corking the Black and Baltic Seas and preventing "the development of the maximum submarine effort around the North Cape." "Monty" theorized that if NATO's flanks were lost while the center held, defeat would become inevitable. Conversely, if NATO secured the flanks, it could regain the initiative despite the loss of the center.[10]

Indeed, NATO planned for operations on the European periphery. Exercises, such as Mainbrace in 1952, included carrier strikes in support of ground forces around Bodo and Narvik in northern Norway, as well as antisurface and ASW operations off the coast.[11]

Although the U.S. Navy had long favored operations on the flanks, the focus on northern waters represented a shift from the Mediterranean as the primary European area of operations during a war. American adherence to the North Atlantic Treaty, the Navy's capabilities to operate in Arctic regions, and the Soviet buildup in the Kola Peninsula directed the strategic focus northward.

Nevertheless, Sherman's early reluctance to operate in Arctic waters influenced Navy planning long after his death.[12] Burke noted that for all the talk about Arctic operations over the years, the Navy was woefully short of detailed information about the area. He wrote that

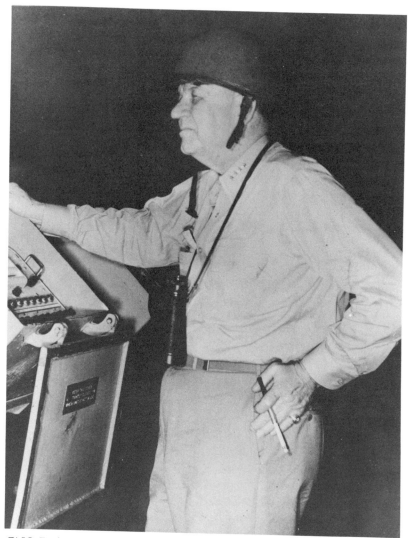

CNO Fechteler observes shore bombardment on board the battleship *Iowa* off Wonsan, North Korea, in August 1952. (NH 49543)

"during the period 1855 through 1937 more marine observations were obtained in the sea area about Little America [in Antarctica] than in the Barents Sea." Burke questioned whether the Navy had "sufficient accurate weather information to plan effectively for carrier task group operations in this area of notoriously foul weather."[13]

Rear Admiral Arleigh A.
Burke, head of the Strategic
Plans Division, November
1952. (80-G-K-14357)

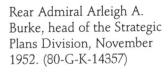By 1953 the Strategic Plans Division began to adjust to the northern strategy. An October 1953 study concluded:

> The Northeast Atlantic-Norwegian Sea-Barents Sea area may well
> be the area of decision with respect to the success of any United
> States operations to maintain the flow of supplies to our European
> Allies and to our U.S. forces in Western Europe. This area is of two
> fold importance—first as an avenue for the movement of U.S. ship-
> ping: secondly, as the area from which the Soviet submarine threat
> may be stopped at its source. Our strongest European ally is the
> United Kingdom. . . . There can be no question about Allied con-
> trol of the sea lanes to the United Kingdom if British forces are to
> be kept in the war. [T]he United Kingdom . . . is the keystone of all
> U.S.-Western European strategy. Of further importance is the fact
> that the northwestern and northern coasts of Norway are extremely
> attractive sites for submarine bases. The fjords are ideal places to
> construct sub pens tunneled into cliffs rising from the sea. Were the
> Soviet to capture these coastal areas by amphibious operations,
> they could construct submarine bases in the fjords that would be
> all but invulnerable to air attack. Another critical aspect of this area
> is the fact that the Barents Sea is the attack route to the only signifi-
> cant submarine base for Atlantic submarines now available to the
> Soviets. With the Bosphorus and Baltic exits sealed, Soviet sub-
> marines must be operated from their northern bases.[14]

The strategic debate over the conduct of a potential third world
war marked a continuation of the struggle fought by Denfeld and

Sherman with the Army and Air Force over the missions assigned the Navy in the European theater. But the admission of Greece and Turkey into NATO and the doubling of the size of the U.S. Navy between 1949 and 1952 made the issue less critical, for the former insured a naval mission to the eastern Mediterranean, and the latter enabled the Navy to plan operations in both the northeastern Atlantic and the Mediterranean.[15] Serious consideration of Norwegian and Barents Sea operations in the early 1950s gave the Navy, in the European theater at least, a concept that truly resembles that of the 1980s.

◆ ◆ ◆

The Navy's maritime strategy, so diligently developed in OPNAV between 1946 and 1952, was lost during the presidency of Dwight D. Eisenhower and the tours of two successive Chiefs of Naval Operations—Admirals Robert B. Carney and Arleigh A. Burke. By the end of Eisenhower's second term, the Navy's strategic concept had become so diffused that it was barely recognizable.

Many factors undermined the Navy's postwar strategy: the service's failure to gain recognition for the concept as a discrete element of the national strategy; the subordination of the Navy's world view which accompanied unification of the armed forces; changing strategic imperatives worldwide; the technological evolution of the weapons of war; and the growing involvement of the United States in regional conflicts.

Admiral Robert B. Carney, Chief of Naval Operations, 1954. (NH 83604)

Admiral Burke relieves Admiral Carney as CNO, while Secretary of the Navy Charles S. Thomas looks on, 17 August 1955. (80-G-669741)

In contrast with the Navy's efforts during the 1980s to disseminate its Maritime Strategy as widely as possible, the service in the late 1940s and early 1950s failed to develop the broad public support necessary to sustain a strategic concept. Neither Sherman nor his successors followed through on suggestions to develop a declassified form of the presentation he so often made during 1947.[16] The strategic concept was enunciated only in highly classified plans and supporting documents which received limited circulation even within the Navy. Naval leaders, especially Sherman, were concerned about compromising national security.[17]

But Sherman did come to appreciate the need to market the Navy more widely and to formulate a maritime strategic concept independent of the war plans. He was much more vocal and public as CNO about Navy intentions than he had been as DCNO. Before his death, Sherman approved the establishment of a course on advanced strategy and sea power at the Naval War College in Newport, Rhode Island.[18]

Captain J. C. Wylie, who headed the effort, saw the new program as a means to dispel the "confusion" and "internal contradictions" that had surfaced during the unification hearings concerning the Navy, its strategy, and sea power.[19] He hoped to "educate our own people" as to why the United States needed a navy in the postwar period: control of the sea had become not the final objective, but a means to an end—the extension ashore, in peacetime and wartime, of the military, political, economic, diplomatic, and psychological aspects of national power.[20] To publicize the Navy's strategic concept beyond the War College, Wylie offered his services and those of his staff as speech writers. He proposed using contacts at fleet commands to influence and regularize the approach to naval operations written into planning documents.[21]

In a parallel effort, Wylie entered the U.S. Naval Institute's prize essay contest of 1953 and won an honorable mention for his piece, appropriately entitled "On Maritime Strategy." Wylie concluded:

> A maritime strategy is one in which the world's maritime communications systems are exploited as the main avenues by way of which strength may be applied to establish control over one's enemies.
>
> Maritime strategy normally consists of two major phases. The first, and it must be first, is the establishment of control of the sea. After an adequate control of the sea is gained comes the second phase, the exploitation of that control by projection of power into one or more selected critical areas of decision on land.[22]

Wylie considered his emphasis on the extension of sea power ashore "a first," and until Huntington published "National Policy and the Transoceanic Navy" the following year, no better public formulation of the Navy's postwar strategy appeared.[23]

Although Wylie's War College endeavors ended when he returned to sea in 1953, the captain continued his efforts.[24] While head of the Naval Warfare Plans Section of the Strategic Plans Division, Wylie published in the August 1957 issue of the *Proceedings,* "Why a Sailor Thinks Like a Sailor." He reiterated the general principles enunciated in his "On Maritime Strategy."[25]

Burke also appreciated the need to disseminate a clearly stated strategic concept.

> It all comes back to the basic principle of a good command philosophy in any organization, the necessity to have the basic concept of naval warfare and the control of naval forces widely promulgated

so that everybody knew it, so that all naval commands would understand and support them.[26]

As head of the Strategic Plans Division, Burke generated, by his own reckoning, "voluminous" correspondence, pulling together the concepts that would guide planning and operations. Unfortunately, the efforts of Burke and Wylie came too late.[27]

The Navy's failure between 1946 and 1953 to develop an identifiable strategic concept separate from joint plans all but assured the demise of its postwar strategic concept. The Defense Department Reorganization Plan 6 of April 1953 strengthened the powers of the Secretary of Defense, the Chairman of the Joint Chiefs of Staff, his secretariat, and the unified commanders. Thereafter, the influence of the individual services in the planning process diminished further.[28] After 1953, the Joint Staff "dictated" how plans would be prepared at all levels, a change that "screwed up," in Wylie's view, the very sensible planning structure developed by the Navy before the Second World War.[29] A comparison of plans completed before 1951, such as Dropshot and Offtackle, with those completed after 1954 reveals how the change in the method of preparation adversely affected the presentation of the Navy's concept of naval warfare. The post-1953 generation of war plans diluted the Navy's vision of how it would fight a war and dispersed myriad tasks among the three services.

(A new strategic environment, altered by the advent of new technology, also contributed to the demise of the Navy's clearly defined strategic concept. The Eisenhower administration considered nuclear weapons, available in relatively great numbers by 1953, an economical alternative to large standing conventional forces and the most effective way to overwhelm an adversary. Concepts such as the "New Look" and "Massive Retaliation" affected the Navy in several ways.[30] First, the fleet's primary weapon systems, the aircraft carrier task forces, were reoriented towards the nuclear strike role.[31] Second, the shift towards nuclear warfare, which limited the Navy to strikes against Soviet maritime targets, undermined the more traditional naval missions. The director of the Navy's Operations Evaluation Group observed that

> changes in aircraft complements anticipated for future attack carrier air groups may have a large influence on ability to supply specific offensive effort. In particular, if a given fraction of effort is to be maintained for defensive purposes; (a) Although the number of

Admiral Radford meets with President-elect Eisenhower, 13 December 1952. (80-G-629194)

sorties will tend to increase as all-jet complements are approached, the ordnance delivery capabilities (conventional weapons) may very well decrease, especially for longer range strikes; (b) An even more drastic change in the ability to maintain aircraft over a battle-field will result; close support capabilities may easily be reduced by a factor as large as 8 or 10, and may, in fact, for certain combat radii of interest, almost completely disappear.[32]

Although the Navy's adaptation to the "New Look" guaranteed its survival during the Eisenhower era, the emphasis on nuclear warfare contributed significantly to the loss of the strategic concept developed during the first postwar years. Carrier task forces, armed with nuclear strike bombers and dispersed for atomic survival—rather than concentrated for forward, offensive operations—made the execution of a conventional maritime strategy problematic.

The development and planning that began in the early 1950s for an ocean-floor Sound Surveillance System (SOSUS) further eroded the Navy's strategic concept. SOSUS systems, as ultimately deployed years later, monitored the movements of Soviet submarines. The most important segment ultimately would become that established in the North Atlantic bottom along the Greenland-Iceland-United Kingdom (G-I-UK) Gap.

Initially, SOSUS was to be the third line of defense in a wartime ASW campaign against the Soviet Union. SOSUS would identify those submarines that left their bases before forward operations went into effect or that subsequently evaded NATO forces. Specialist ASW forces would form the second line of defense north of the Gap. American carriers, submarines, and minelaying forces would operate directly against Soviet submarine bases in the Kola Peninsula and form the first line of defense.

The SOSUS system in the G-I-UK Gap was never intended to be the primary line of defense that many consider it to be. It was to be part of a North Atlantic system of defense in depth. As with many "walls" constructed over the centuries, once built, it could become an attractive fall-back position behind which an armed force could operate comfortably in peacetime, but unsuccessfully in wartime. The construction of the SOSUS line led to the development of a "SOSUS-mentality," as stiflingly defensive as the "Maginot Mentality" that gripped the French Army in the 1930s.

Another technological development, Soviet deployment of nuclear-powered guided missile submarines (SSGNs) late in the 1950s, reinforced this defensive-mindedness. During the late 1940s, Soviet submarines that would have evaded destruction in offensive operations were capable only of sinking Allied ships. But Soviet SSGNs loose off the Atlantic coast would be incinerating American cities, not simply sending merchant ships to the bottom. As CNO, planning for a war that everyone assumed would be nuclear, Admiral Burke had little choice but to attempt to track and to target every Soviet SSGN operating within range of the United States. While he still intended to conduct forward, offensive operations against Soviet submarine bases, he increasingly adopted defensive plans and deployments to counter the SSGN threat.[33]

The changing situation in Asia also contributed to the ruin of the Navy's postwar strategic concept. Sherman and his planners had visualized direct operations against the Soviet Union in the Far East, where neither the geographic bulwarks of the Balkan and Anatolian peninsulas nor the Arctic weather of the Barents Sea posed barriers. But the ability of the Navy to concentrate its forces against the Soviet territories in East Asia quickly evaporated. The fall of China to the Communists in 1949 expanded the potential theater for hostile operations throughout the Western Pacific. Budget cuts further reduced forces available for offensive operations. Crises in Southeast Asia and concern for Taiwan's security held the Navy's attention for another two decades. As a consequence, from 1953 to 1975 the Navy was unable to focus on the Soviet threat in the Pacific as it had between 1946 and 1953.

◆ ◆ ◆

In retrospect, the United States Navy made a remarkable and rapid transition from an "oceanic" to a "transoceanic" strategy during the first postwar decade. Its strategic concept took on the essential forms associated with the Maritime Strategy of the 1980s. The Navy prepared to fight a global, protracted war; to take the offensive from the start with the forces at hand. In the Mediterranean in 1946 the Navy demonstrated its understanding of the relationship between forward operations and American national interests, not just in wartime, but in peacetime. A balanced fleet stood prepared for all contingencies, from routine naval presence deployments to global nuclear war. The Navy's operations abroad, both in Europe and Asia, highlighted American commitment to the defense of allies and served as a visible deterrent to the Soviet Union and other potential enemies.

There are differences, of course, between the Navy's strategy of the first postwar decade and the Maritime Strategy of the 1980s. The Navy's postwar planners remained wedded to a "swing" strategy, moving carrier task forces from the Pacific to the Atlantic in wartime, a concept since discarded. The Maritime Strategy has been well publicized and subjected to open debate. The Navy's original postwar strategic concept was cloaked in secrecy.

That there are differences between the Navy's early and current strategies should be expected; that those differences are so limited is remarkable. The strategic planning process is a dynamic one. Plans are constantly altered and updated as circumstances change. The most obvious transformation has been the development since the 1960s of a powerful Soviet surface navy. Despite that buildup, the Russian surface fleet remains but a tertiary threat, just as in the late 1940s and the early 1950s when the Navy considered the Soviet subsurface and air threats of primary and secondary importance, respectively. Anti-submarine warfare remains, in the words of Admiral Trost, *"the Mother Lode"* of the U.S. Navy.[34] And who can say that well into a global and protracted Soviet-American war, carriers would not be shifted from one ocean to the other if circumstances warranted such a "swing"?

That the late 1970s witnessed the rediscovery of a strategic concept enunciated thirty years earlier by Vice Admiral Forrest Sherman should come as no surprise. The establishment of diplomatic relations between the United States and the People's Republic of China during the Carter administration and the perception of that nation's growing opposition to the Soviet Union allowed the U.S. Navy, as it had between 1946 and 1949, to focus on the Soviet threat in the northeastern Pacific. As an appropriate response, the Pacific Fleet in 1977 under Admiral Hayward produced Sea Strike, the recognized precursor of the Maritime Strategy. The development of the Polaris and Trident-armed American ballistic missile submarines, the U.S. Navy's primary sea-based strategic nuclear platforms, freed the service's aircraft carriers for other missions. The increase in the range of Soviet ballistic missile submarines and their withdrawal to bastions in Arctic waters once again drew attention to the far northern seas of both the Atlantic and Pacific. These factors, combined with the expectation that a Soviet-American war would remain conventional, in its initial stages at least, recreated conditions under which the Navy three decades before had developed a rational response—a maritime strategy—*The Maritime Strategy*.

Appendix

Presentation to the President
14 January 1947
Vice Admiral Forrest Sherman, U.S. Navy,
Deputy Chief of Naval Operations (Operations)

Mr. President:

It is our purpose, this afternoon, to present as briefly as possible our estimate of the probable character of a major war in the next few years; the tasks of the Navy in such a war; the ships, aircraft, bases, and personnel needed now to permit the Navy to act as an effective deterrent against such a war, and to function effectively if it should occur.

Our naval estimates are of necessity derived from strategic concepts arrived at by joint Army and Navy agencies, and I shall, therefore, present many of those joint strategic concepts during this discussion.

For reasons with which you are familiar, we consider that Russia is our most probable enemy and that in the event of war in the near future we would, at least initially, have Great Britain as an ally. We do not believe that Russia desires such a war, but we do believe that weakness on our part, militarily or diplomatically, might lead to Soviet aggression which would lead to an unlimited war. Accordingly we believe it is sound to base our military and naval establishments on our concepts of such a war.

Our intelligence indicates that the Soviets have a capability of mobilizing up to 10 million men within 30 days and reaching a peak of 15 million in 150 days. Mobilization in this instance can mean little more than bringing the men under military control with but very limited initial effectiveness.

We estimate that next summer the Russians will have a little over three million men in some 208 ground divisions; an Air Force of 13,000 combat aircraft manned by 550,000 men; and a Navy of 300,000 men manning between 700 and 800 ships and craft, most of them of low combat value except for submarines and motor torpedo boats.

It is possible that within two years the Russians might be able to send an appreciable number of one way flights of bombers against the northern United States, using aircraft similar to our present B-17's or B-24's, or possibly our B-29's. Long range guided missiles based on German design are now in the hands of the Russians. However, we do not believe that Russia will be able to conduct any major bombing or guided missile operations or to mount significant airborne troops operations against the United States proper for at least a decade provided we deny the Russians the use of Iceland, Greenland, and Alaska.

Except for a submarine force, the Soviets will not be able to create an effective high seas naval force with offensive capabilities for many years. Russia is believed to have 213 submarines of all types. The 1947 annual building capability of Russian developed types is estimated at 50 fleet submarines, principally at Leningrad-Kronstadt, Molotovsk (on the White Sea), Nicolaev and Sevastopol (on the Black Sea), and Vladivostok. It is believed that the Soviets are devoting great effort to the building of the German Type XXI submarine. As you will recall, Mr. President, that is the type of submarine in which you dove during your recent visit to Key West. As you will also recall, it was developed by the Germans shortly before V-E Day and because it is of such high submerged speed and so quiet running, it is a great potential danger to us. German submarine building plants have been awarded the Soviets as reparations and they have moved crews, workmen, and engineers into Russia. Former German assembly yards at Danzig, Elbing, Gdynia and Koenigsberg are in the hands of the Russians. Initially the Soviets could probably maintain 40 submarines at sea in the Atlantic; 30 in the Pacific; and, after the Dardanelles have been opened, 18 in the Mediterranean. For purposes of comparison, during the first nine months of the past war, Germany maintained an average of only 6 submarines in the Atlantic which sank nearly two million tons of shipping. These submarines would be a serious threat to our sea communications and could be a significant handicap to our naval and amphibious operations.

The Russian Navy is divided between the Far East, the White Sea, the Baltic and the Black Sea. In the four areas there are deployed in forces of approximately equal strength a total of four battleships, eleven cruisers, fifty-eight destroyers, forty-five destroyer escorts, over two hundred submarines, and the several hundred amphibious, mine, patrol, and auxiliary types which constitute the Russian Navy.

Our joint planning and intelligence agencies estimate that in the event of a major war, Russia would initiate immediate operations to overrun Germany, France, Belgium, Holland, and Denmark; and would initiate attacks on Great Britain with aircraft, with rockets and guided missiles, with submarines, and with mines; and for defensive reasons would overrun and occupy portions of the Scandinavian Peninsula.

The Russian decision with respect to attack on Spain would depend on developments. Distance and tenuous land communications would make the operation a difficult one. However, occupation of Spain would close the Straits of Gibraltar to us.

We estimate that Russia would attempt to seize the Middle East and its oil; occupy Turkey, Greece, and Italy in order to control the Mediterranean; and eventually would attempt to control the Suez Canal. These operations in southern Europe and the Middle East might precede those in northern Europe and might be initiated by satellite countries.

In the Far East, we believe Russian operations would be limited to seizing Manchuria, Korea, and North China.

It seems probable that from the present deployments of her forces, Russian offensives would be launched westward through Germany and Western Europe to use the Atlantic or North Sea coast, and concurrently southward through the Middle East and to the Mediterranean.

The ability of the United States to stop such offensives, and to initiate counter-offensives, would depend: on our prior planning and preparation; on our appreciation of the approach of war; on support given to our potential allies; and on our degree of readiness.

Our joint concepts envisage that the principle initial counter-offensive efforts against Russia itself would consist of a strategic air offensive from bases in the British Isles and in the vicinity of Suez, and perhaps from India. Concurrently operations would be conducted to secure the British Isles, Iceland and the Azores, to keep the Mediterranean open, and to advance ground and air forces northward into the Black Sea region.

For us, a counter-offensive against Russia through the Mediterranean is preferable to one through Western Europe because it permits exploitation of our sea, air and amphibious strength in which we can be vastly superior.

Holding the Mediterranean involves the maximum use of our combined resources to assist Spain and Turkey, and to secure positions which dominate the Mediterranean line of communications. The British Isles must be defended, and would require substantial assistance from us; but we believe that the Mediterranean would become the defensive theater of war. We recognize that, as time passes, and particularly if Russian political objectives change, the Far East may become the area in which a war is more likely to start. Should such a development occur, it would dictate a shift in our deployments toward the Pacific and strengthening of the defense of Alaska.

In the event of war with Russia, the naval tasks we currently consider most essential are:

a. To protect the United States;
b. To control essential sea and air communications;
c. To evacuate our occupation forces from Europe;
d. To assist in protecting the United Kingdom;
e. To assist in holding Japan and in providing for the safety of our forces in China and Korea;
f. To assist in retarding Soviet advances into Norway, Spain, Italy, Greece and Turkey, and towards Suez;
g. To place the Army Air Forces in positions to initiate our air offensive as soon as possible;
h. To prevent Soviet use of sea communications; and
i. To seize and defend positions from which subsequent offensives may be launched.

We envisage that from the naval point of view such a war would have four distinct phases.

The *first phase* would be one of initial operations by our existing forces, of stabilization of the Soviet offensive, and of mobilization and preparation of additional forces, and of expansion of production of war material. The nation would be on the strategic defensive but our naval and air forces should assume the offensive immediately in order to secure our own sea communications, support our forces overseas, disrupt enemy operations, and force dissipation of enemy strength. In this phase the Navy would have a tremendous initial responsibility. Early offensive blows would be of extreme importance in shortening the war.

During this phase the Reserve Fleets would be activated as expeditiously as possible in order to provide our minimum requirements. For the Atlantic these include a carrier task force of 16 carriers with suitable supporting ships, and for the Pacific approximately half that number. Strong submarine forces would be required for such tasks as destruction of enemy controlled shipping, reconnaissance, and inshore work, sea-air rescue, patrol of advanced areas and bottling up the Russian Navy. Our active amphibious forces and Fleet Marine Force should be ready with naval-air and gunfire support to move promptly to occupy advance bases. Anti-submarine operations would commence immediately. Appropriate vessels would promptly initiate movement of Army aircraft and supplies to the British Isles, the Middle East, and other critical positions. Meanwhile expansion of the Navy would proceed, with emphasis on readiness of amphibious forces and shipping being integrated with readiness of Army forces.

Specific targets for early carrier attacks might include objectives in Manchuria, North Korea and Siberia to cover the withdrawal of our forces from Korea and North China; and objectives in northwest Germany and in northern Italy to cover the retirement of our occupation forces.

Our submarines would be deployed promptly to bottle up the Russian forces in the Far East, the White Sea, the Baltic and the Black Sea and to patrol the approaches to Alaska and the Aleutians.

Anti-submarine measures would be initiated promptly along the routes over which our troops and vital shipping must pass.

The *second phase* would be one of progressive reduction of Soviet war potential and build-up of our own. Operations would be characterized first by increased offensive action by naval and air forces and by joint forces, and subsequently by general advancement of our base areas as our military power permits. During this phase, large elements of all services would be moved overseas; advanced bases would be established and stocked; and requirements for shipping of all sorts and for naval escorts would increase rapidly.

The *third phase* would involve a continued and sustained bombing offensive. The Dardanelles would be opened and limited positions seized in Europe and in the Middle East as desired. Naval activity would consist of maintaining our overseas lines of communications,

protection of troop movements, gunfire support for amphibious landings, carrier action against appropriate objectives, and submarine
operations to prevent enemy use of coastal waters.

The *final phase* would comprise the systematic destruction of Soviet industry, internal transportation systems, and general war potential. As naval targets disappeared, our naval operations would become more thoroughly integrated with ground and air operations;
the need for maintenance of heavy carrier striking forces would decrease; while the need for ships for transporting forces and supplies,
and for close-in escort and support would remain high.

Preliminary joint estimates, agreed on at the planning level, as to
requirements for naval forces for the third phase of the war include
carrier task forces built around 24 carriers, amphibious assault lift for
seven divisions plus support ships, and include correspondingly large
escort, anti-submarine, and mine forces.

We estimate that the Merchant Marine would consist initially of
ten million DWT of cargo shipping (1000 ships) manned and operating plus thirty million DWT (3000 ships) laid up. Based on estimated
shipping space required and estimated submarine sinkings, we would
need fifty million DWT (5000 ships). Hence the mobilization of the
Merchant Marine would require the manning and activation of 3000
ships (30 million DWT) and the building, equipping and manning of
another 1000 vessels in the first two years of the war.

From the foregoing, we derive our basic naval requirements, which
are:

a. Amphibious forces with which to transport troops to overseas
   positions and land them against opposition;
b. Carrier air forces which are the only means of providing a highly
   effective mobile tactical air force at sea or in coastal areas distant
   from our own prepared air bases—and which can serve as a
   striking force for the destruction of specific targets;
c. Surface fighting ships to support the amphibious forces and
   carrier forces and to furnish gunfire support for amphibious
   landings;
d. Submarine forces of great power and a high degree of technological development;
e. Anti-submarine and naval reconnaissance forces, surface and air
   capable of effectively covering the approaches to our coasts and
   our essential supply lines at sea and of covering and supporting
   our ships;

f. Supply ships and auxiliaries for the logistical support of all forces overseas, including the land armies and land air forces.

Our basic naval establishment plan is designed to retain and deploy active fleets in such a manner as to ready them for war requirements and at the same time to accomplish their essential peacetime tasks. We will now show a series of cards which list for the principal active naval commands the peacetime tasks, the forces available, and the initial war tasks together with our naval base system needed to support them. They also show the Reserve Fleets which are being preserved to permit prompt naval expansion if ever required. The current tasks assigned are derived of course from the recent unified command directive.

With the passage of time and the expected development of aircraft and airborne missiles, the importance of the northern approaches to the United States will increase. We anticipate that naval forces will be called on to operate in the Arctic regions to seize and support bases for our air forces, and to prevent the use of the Arctic regions as bases for attack against us. For that reason we are grasping every opportunity to increase our skill in cold weather operations and to improve our material for such service. . . .

Notes

All primary sources cited in this study are held by the Operational Archives Branch of the Naval Historical Center in Washington, D.C. While the sources indicated in the notes should be apparent, short forms and corresponding full citations include:

JCS—Papers of the CNO Secretariat
00 File—Records of the Immediate Office of the CNO
OP-23—Records of the Organizational Research and
    Policy Division
Strategic Plans—Strategic Plans Division Records (OP-30)
Command File—Post 1 January 1946 Command File
Plans File—Post 1 January 1946 Plans File
Report File—Post 1 January 1946 Report File

Introduction

1. See Robert W. Komer's *Maritime Strategy or Coalition Defense?* (Cambridge, MA, 1984). In chapters 6 and 7, Komer associates the Maritime Strategy with the Reagan/Lehman 600-ship Navy and ignores the fact that the debate began midway through the Carter administration when Komer was Under Secretary of Defense for Policy (1979–1981).

2. Carlisle A. H. Trost, "Looking Beyond the Maritime Strategy," U.S. Naval Institute *Proceedings* (hereafter cited as *Proceedings*) 113 (Jan 1987): 15.

3. Harlan K. Ullman, "The Pacific and US Naval Policy," *Naval Forces* 6 (Jun 1985): 40; and John B. Hattendorf, "The Evolution of the Maritime Strategy: 1977 to 1987," *Naval War College Review* 41 (Summer 1988): 7–38.

4. House Committee on Armed Services, *Hearings on Military Posture and H.R. 1872 [S. 4040], Department of Defense Authorization for Appropria-*

tions for Fiscal Year 1980 and H.R. 2575 [S. 4291], Department of Defense Supplemental Authorization for Appropriations for Fiscal Year 1979 before the Seapower and Strategic and Critical Materials Subcommittee, pt. 4, 96th Cong., 1st sess., 1979, pp. 37–71. Hayward's opening statement appeared as "The Future of U.S. Sea Power," *Proceedings* 105 (May 1979): 66–71.

5. Ibid., p. 41.

6. Richard Hart Sinnreich, "Strategic Implications for Doctrinal Change: A Case Analysis," in Keith A. Dunn and William O. Staudenmaier, eds., *Military Strategy in Transition: Defense and Deterrence in the 1980s* (Boulder and London, 1984), pp. 43–46.

7. Ibid., p. 46. For an example of the call within the Army for a new doctrine, see Wayne A. Downing, "US Army Operations Doctrine: A Challenge for the 1980s and Beyond," *Military Review* 51 (Jan 1981): 64–73.

8. Ibid., p. 48. The Army's AirLand Battle doctrine, like the Maritime Strategy, is criticized for eroding deterrence, lowering the nuclear threshold, and potentially making possible a NATO offensive posture—a land warfare form of "horizontal escalation"—that might be directed against the Soviet Union's Warsaw Pact allies. See Samuel P. Huntington, "Conventional Deterrence and Conventional Retaliation in Europe," pp. 23–28; and Boyd Sutton et al., "Strategic and Doctrinal Implications of Deep Attack Concepts for the Defense of Central Europe," pp. 66–69, 71–74, in Dunn and Staudenmaier, eds., *Military Strategy in Transition.*

9. Ibid., pp. 48–49. Sinnreich refers here to the 1982 version of FM 100-5.

10. Peter M. Swartz, "Contemporary U.S. Naval Strategy: A Bibliography," *Proceedings* 112 (Jan 1986 Supplement): 41.

11. Samuel P. Huntington, "National Policy and the Transoceanic Navy," *Proceedings* 80 (May 1954): 488, 491–92.

12. Ibid., pp. 483–84.

13. John J. Mearsheimer, "A Strategic Misstep: The Maritime Strategy and Deterrence in Europe," *International Security* 11 (Fall 1986): 5–42, and passim. For another critical view of the Maritime Strategy see Jack Beatty, "In Harm's Way," *The Atlantic Monthly* 259 (May 1987): 37–53.

14. James D. Watkins, "The Maritime Strategy," *Proceedings* 112 (Jan 1986 Supplement): 4.

15. Linton F. Brooks, "Naval Power and National Security: The Case for the Maritime Strategy," *International Security* 11 (Fall 1986): 59.

16. Trost, "Looking Beyond the Maritime Strategy," p. 15.

Chapter 1. The Challenge of Victory

1. Stefan T. Possony, "The Vindication of Sea Power," *Proceedings* 71 (Sep 1945): 1033–43.

2. Bernard Brodie, "New Tactics in Naval Warfare," *Foreign Affairs* 24 (Jan 1946): 210–23.

3. "Mitchellites" derived their name from Brigadier General William "Billy" Mitchell, the interwar proponent of strategic air power who argued, and attempted to demonstrate in attacks on unmanned, stationary battleships, that air power had made navies obsolescent.

4. Extreme proponents of unification envisioned the Air Force and the Army absorbing the Navy's air and amphibious components respectively. The Navy would retain only the submarine force—the third pillar of its Pacific victory.

5. James Forrestal, address at Princeton University, 20 Sept 1942 in *New York Times,* 21 Sep 1942, p. 11; Harley Cope, "When Peace Comes," *Proceedings* 69 (Feb 1943): 165–68; H. H. Smith-Hutton, "Post-War Problems and the Navy," *Proceedings* 69 (Jun 1943): 785–93; Hanson W. Baldwin, "Shall We Police the World?" *Sea Power* 4 (Mar 1944): 6–8; Ashley Halsey, Jr., "A Slide-Rule Formula for a Post-War Navy," *Proceedings* 70 (Apr 1944): 371–84; James Forrestal, "Keep the Navy to Keep the Peace," *Sea Power* 5 (Jul 1945): 21–22.

6. Michael Vlahos, *Blue Sword: The Naval War College and the American Mission, 1919–1941* (Newport, RI, 1980), pp. 113–30.

7. For Huntington's discussion of the "phases" of American naval history see "National Policy and the Transoceanic Navy," pp. 485–90.

8. Ibid., p. 484.

9. American and Allied amphibious operations in the European theater during the Second World War were "transoceanic" by definition. Nevertheless, the Navy was quick to turn its back on Europe and focus, as it had before the war, on the Pacific.

10. Knox's speech, quoted in Vincent Davis, *Postwar Defense Policy and the U.S. Navy, 1943–1946* (Chapel Hill, 1962), p. 27. See also Baldwin, "Shall We Police the World?" p. 6.

11. Forrestal, "Keep the Navy," p. 21.

12. Alarmed by intelligence in July 1943 that indicated the Army was already drafting postwar proposals, the Navy Department hastily launched into the process itself for fear of losing a march to the Army. Fleet Admiral Ernest J. King, COMINCH/CNO, ordered the establishment of a planning section within the CNO staff. Davis, *Postwar Defense Policy,* p. 13. For another study of wartime planning see Michael S. Sherry, *Preparing for the Next War: American Plans for Postwar Defense, 1941–1945* (New Haven and London, 1977).

13. Daniel Yergin, *Shattered Peace: The Origins of the Cold War and the National Security State* (Boston, 1977), pp. 193–94.

14. Davis, *Postwar Defense Policy,* pp. 4–79; and Sherry, *Preparing for the Next War,* pp. 32–35.

15. Davis, *Postwar Defense Policy,* pp. 41–63; and Yergin, *Shattered Peace,* pp. 201–204.

16. This is not to imply that the Eastern Atlantic or the Mediterranean were unfamiliar to the U.S. Navy. The American naval presence in the Mediterranean dated back to 1800, and the Navy operated in European waters in both world wars. Nevertheless, naval war planning before 1945 focused on the Western Atlantic and the Pacific.

17. Davis, *Postwar Defense Policy,* pp. 33–35.

18. Ibid., p. 85. Forrestal was officially appointed secretary on 18 May and was sworn in the following day.

19. Forrestal, address before the Maryland Historical Society, 10 May 1943, quoted in Sherry, *Preparing for the Next War,* p. 33.

20. Forrestal made the call in his address to the graduating class of the U.S. Naval Academy, Annapolis, MD, on 7 June 1944; quoted in Davis, *Postwar Defense Policy,* pp. 84–85.

21. Forrestal, "Keep the Navy," p. 21. See also U.S. Requirements for Post-War Air Bases, 10 Jan 1944, JCS 570/2.

22. Davis, *Postwar Defense Policy,* pp. 101–102; Yergin, *Shattered Peace,* pp. 208–209.

23. Ibid., pp. 35–38, 194, 204–206. See also Lynn Etheridge Davis, *The Cold War Begins: Soviet-American Conflict over Eastern Europe* (Princeton, 1974); and Hugh De Santis, *The Diplomacy of Silence: The American Foreign Service, the Soviet Union, and the Cold War* (Chicago and London, 1981).

24. Yergin, *Shattered Peace,* pp. 208–209.

25. Davis, *Postwar Defense Policy,* p. 99.

26. Ibid., pp. 102–111.

27. Total strength would be 665,000.

28. Davis, *Postwar Defense Policy,* pp. 104–110; Basic Post-War Plan No. 1, 7 May 1945, COMINCH/CNO, World War II Plans File.

29. Davis, *Postwar Defense Policy,* p. 165.

30. Mitscher to Forrestal, 24 Sep 1945, no. 4, Series I, DCNO (Air).

31. King to SECNAV, 5 Nov 1945, enclosing Hill to King, 29 Oct; Blandy to King, 18 Oct; and Radford to King, 29 Oct, Basic Post-War Plan No. 1A, 14 Dec 1945, COMINCH/CNO, WW II Plans File.

32. Emphasis in the original.

33. King to SECNAV, 5 Nov 1945, enclosing Hill to King, 29 Oct; Blandy to King, 18 Oct; and Radford to King, 29 Oct; and Basic Post-War Plan No. 1A, 14 Dec 1945, COMINCH/CNO, WW II Plans.

34. Ibid. Emphasis in the original.

Chapter 2. A Prospective Enemy

1. Arnold Wolfers, *Discord and Collaboration: Essays on International Politics* (Baltimore, 1962), pp. 48, 58, 190–91, 205–206.

2. Edward M. Bennett, *Franklin D. Roosevelt and the Search for Security: American-Soviet Relations, 1933–1939* (Wilmington, DE, 1985), pp. 8–10.

3. If built, the battleship would have been larger than the United States' own *Iowa*-class. The administration eventually scaled-down its recommendation to a 45,000-ton warship with 16-inch guns. The Navy resisted all such efforts to aid the Soviet Union. See Thomas R. Maddux, "United States-Soviet Naval Relations in the 1930's: The Soviet Union's Efforts to Purchase Naval Vessels," *Naval War College Review* 29 (Fall 1976): 33–35; and Malcolm Muir, Jr., "American Warship Construction for Stalin's Navy Prior to World War II: A Study in Paralysis of Policy," *Diplomatic History* 5 (Fall 1981): 337–51.

4. John Lewis Gaddis, *The Long Peace: Inquiries into the History of the Cold War* (New York and Oxford, 1987), p. 26.

5. Quoted in Robert E. Sherwood, *Roosevelt and Hopkins: An Intimate History* (New York, 1948), p. 923. For Hopkin's sense of impending deterioration in Soviet-American relations see the record of his conversations with Stalin during his final trip to Moscow in ibid., pp. 887,–912; and Charles E. Bohlen's *Witness to History, 1929–1967* (New York, 1973), p. 222.

6. Looking back at the origins of containment, George F. Kennan writes: "And what I was trying to say . . . was simply this: 'Don't make any more unnecessary concessions to these people. Make it clear to them that they are not going to be allowed to establish any dominant influence in Western Europe and in Japan if there is anything we can do to prevent it. When we have stabilized the situation in this way, then perhaps we will be able to talk with them about some sort of general political and military disengagement in Europe and the Far East—not before." George F. Kennan, "Containment Then and Now," *Foreign Affairs* 65 (Spring 1987): 887.

7. Walter Millis, ed., *The Forrestal Diaries* (New York, 1951), pp. 50–51. Forrestal copied into his diary Kennan's famous "Long Telegram" of 22 February 1946, and persuaded Kennan to write and publish his famous "X" article. See Forrestal Diaries, 4 vols., 4: 879–93, Privileged Manuscript Collection; Kennan, "The Sources of Soviet Conduct," *Foreign Affairs* 25 (Jul 1947): 572–82; and "Containment Then and Now," pp. 885–86.

8. Captain Stephen Jurika, Jr., a politico/military affairs expert on Vice Admiral Sherman's staff, felt at the time that the State Department was "selling the West down the river." Stephen Jurika, Jr., interview

with John T. Mason, Jr., 1979, 2 vols., 2: 699, U.S. Naval Institute (USNI) Oral History, Annapolis, MD.

9. "Basic Factors in World Relations," report of the ONI, Dec 1945, A-8, box 106, Strategic Plans Division Records (hereafter Strategic Plans).

10. For a good discussion of American Asian policy at the end of the war see Marc S. Gallicchio, *The Cold War Begins in Asia: American East Asian Policy and the Fall of the Japanese Empire* (New York, 1988).

11. CNO to CINCPACFLT, CINCLANTFLT, and COM12FLT, 8 Jan 1946, box 106, Strategic Plans.

12. CINCLANTFLT to CNO, 8 Jan 1946, CINCLANTFLT, Plans File.

13. Bernhard H. Bieri, interview with John T. Mason, Jr., 1970, pp. 277–80, USNI Oral History (hereafter Bieri Oral History); OPLAN 1-46, 20 Jan 1946, COMNAVNAW, Plans File; OPLAN 2-46, 1 Aug 1946, COMNAVMED, Plans File. Bieri complained about lack of direction to Rear Admiral Thomas B. Inglis, head of the Office of Naval Intelligence, during his European tour in the summer of 1946. See "Review of Conditions in Europe" by Inglis before the Navy Department General Planning Group, undated (Fall 1946), A16-3, box 106, Strategic Plans. Bieri's complaints reached Forrestal who promised Bieri closer State-Navy coordination. See Millis, *Forrestal Diaries,* pp. 184–85. While Bieri's recollection was accurate for his first months in the Mediterranean, as the administration formulated its foreign policy during 1946, Bieri received statements of American positions. Bieri's continued pleas for more detailed instructions and his handling of American naval forces in the Mediterranean failed to impress Vice Admiral Sherman during his visit to Naples in August 1946. Sherman returned to Washington determined to upgrade the Mediterranean command structure. He replaced Bieri a year and a half later.

14. Robert Greenhalgh Albion, *Makers of Naval Policy, 1798–1947,* Rowena Reed, ed. (Annapolis, 1980), p. 38. Albion considered Benjamin Stoddert and Gideon Welles the two greatest pre-twentieth-century secretaries of the Navy.

15. Secretary Lehman likewise attracts the attention of most commentators on the modern Navy and too often receives recognition as the originator of the Maritime Strategy to the chagrin of the uniformed Navy.

16. Davis, *Postwar Defense Policy,* pp. 199–201, credits Forrestal with attracting veteran officers back to Washington at war's end but does not list Sherman as a member of Forrestal's "brain trust."

17. House Committee on Naval Affairs, *Sundry Legislation Affecting the Naval Establishment, 1945: Hearing on House Concurrent Resolution 80, Composition of the Postwar Navy,* 79th Cong., 1st sess., 1945, item 110, pp. 1164, 1166–67.

18. Ibid., pp. 1174–75.

19. Ibid., p. 1193.
20. When Mott attempted to question King on why ships of the Italian navy were to be transferred to Russia, Chairman Carl Vinson terminated the discussion. Ibid., p. 1191; Millis, *Forrestal Diaries,* pp. 97–100.
21. JCS 1518, 19 Sep 1945. The study concluded: "Should relations between the major powers break down Russia would present the most difficult problem to resolve from a military point of view." JCS 1518, less the first appendix, "Strategic Concept and Plan for the Employment of United States Armed Forces," formed the basis for SWNCC (State-War-Navy Coordinating Committee) 282. See Thomas H. Etzold and John Lewis Gaddis, eds., *Containment: Documents on American Policy and Strategy, 1945–1950* (New York, 1978), pp. 39–44; and James F. Schnabel, *The History of the Joint Chiefs of Staff: The Joint Chiefs of Staff and National Policy,* vol. 1, *1945–1947* (Washington, 1979), pp. 145–49. Rear Admiral Matthias B. Gardner, a member of OP-30's planning staff, also served on the JPS.
22. JCS 1518, with amendments through JCS 1518/4, 20 Oct 1945, pp. 2–12.
23. JCS 1518, p. 11, as revised; King to JCS, 1 Oct 1945, ibid.
24. Byrnes to the JCS, 6 Mar 1946, JCS 1641.
25. For a recent account of this formative period of the Cold War centering on Churchill's Fulton address, see Fraser J. Harbutt, *The Iron Curtain: Churchill, America, and the Origins of the Cold War* (New York and Oxford, 1986).
26. JCS 1641/1, 10 Mar 1946.
27. JCS to SWNCC, 13 Mar 1946; Leahy to Byrnes, 13 Mar 1946, JCS 1641/3.
28. SWNCC to JCS, 6 Apr 1946, JCS 1641/4. In copy number 3 of JCS 1641/3, sent to CNO Nimitz, someone noted in the margin an "amendment by Mr Acheson" concerning the use the Soviets could make of any unilateral American demands for military bases. Acheson and the Navy Department disagreed over possession of the Mandated islands seized from Japan during the war in the Central Pacific. Acheson favored resolving their fate through the United Nations, but Forrestal argued for United States' retention to prevent a foreign power from taking advantage of their strategic location. See Millis, *Forrestal Diaries,* pp. 130–31.
29. Report of the JPS, 11 Ap 1946, JCS 1641/5.
30. During the Second World War, American strategists had focused on the Northwest European line of operations, that is the cross-channel invasion and the large-scale ground operations in France, the Low Countries, and Germany in an attempt to meet and defeat the major forces of the Third Reich in a decisive campaign.
31. Just as the United States had George Kennan in its Moscow

embassy calling for a tougher line with the Soviets, Britain had Frank Roberts. Roberts considered miscalculation the most probable cause of a Soviet attack. To avoid a Soviet perception that Britain was isolated, he recommended a strong Anglo-American relationship. See Elisabeth Barker, *The British Between the Superpowers, 1945–1950* (Toronto and Buffalo, 1983), pp. 44–45. British politicians foresaw a role for the United States in postwar European affairs. See Forrestal's diary entry for 21 April 1945 concerning his dinner conversation with Anthony Eden in Millis, *Forrestal Diaries,* p. 48.

32. Davis, *Postwar Defense Policy,* p. 178.

33. John Baylis, *Anglo-American Defense Relations, 1939–1984: The Social Relationship,* 2d ed. (New York, 1984), pp. 29–30; Margaret Gowing and Lorna Arnold, *Independence and Deterrence: Britain and Atomic Energy, 1945–1952,* vol. 1, *Policy Making* (London, 1974), pp. 92–94. The Anglo-American atomic connection was likewise strained in the immediate postwar years. See ibid., pp. 95–123.

34. M. S. Anderson, "British Public Opinion and the Russian Campaign of 1812," *Slavonic and East European Review* 34 (Jun 1956): 408–25.

35. Barker, *The British Between the Superpowers,* pp. 6–8, 13. Lord Alanbrooke's diary entry for 27 July 1944 records:

Back to War Office to have an hour with the Secretary of State discussing post-war policy in Europe. Should Germany be dismembered or gradually converted to an ally to meet the Russian threat of twenty years hence? I suggested the latter and feel certain that we must from now onwards regard Germany in a very different light. Germany is no longer the dominating power in Europe— Russia is. . . . Therefore, foster Germany, gradually build her up and bring her into a Federation of Western Europe. . . . Arthur Bryant, *Triumph in the West: A History of the War Years Based on the Diaries of Field-Marshal Lord Alanbrooke, Chief of the Imperial General Staff* (Garden City, NY, 1959), p. 180.

For a historiographic review of the British role in the early Cold War see Jan Melissen and Bert Zeeman, "Britain and western Europe, 1945–51: opportunities lost?" *International Affairs* 63 (Winter 1986/87): 81–95.

36. Ibid., p. 9.

37. Davis, *Postwar Defense Policy,* pp. 76–79; Bieri Oral History, pp. 211–17.

38. Bruce Robellet Kuniholm, *The Origins of the Cold War in the Near East: Great Power Conflict and Diplomacy in Iran, Turkey, and Greece* (Princeton, 1980), pp. 96–97.

39. MacVeagh to Roosevelt, 15 Oct 1944, quoted in ibid., pp. 97–98.

40. Ibid., p. 207.

41. In 1941 when Churchill lamented the loss of the Balkans and set-backs in the Middle East, President Roosevelt played down the British debacle: "There is little of raw materials in all of them put together—not enough to maintain nor compensate for huge occupation forces. The exception is oil." Even the total withdrawal of British forces would matter little in the end. "I say this," Roosevelt wrote, "because I believe the outcome of this struggle is going to be decided in the Atlantic." Roosevelt to Churchill, 1 May and 3 May 1941, in Francis L. Loewenheim, Harold D. Langley, and Manfred Jonas, eds., *Roosevelt and Churchill: Their Secret Wartime Correspondence* (New York, 1975), pp. 138–40, 141.

42. Virtually any book on strategy in the American theater addressed the Anglo-American debate over the extent of Allied commitment in the Mediterranean and the Middle East. For a sound, short study, see Michael Howard, *The Mediterranean Strategy in the Second World War* (New York and Washington, 1968).

43. Quoted in Sherwood, *Roosevelt and Hopkins,* pp. 749–50.

44. Emphasis in the original.

45. Burns to Hopkins, 10 Aug 1943, U.S. Department of State, *Foreign Relations of the United States: The Conferences at Washington and Quebec, 1943* (Washington, 1970), pp. 624–27.

46. McGeorge Bundy, "The Test of Yalta," *Foreign Affairs* 27 (Jul 1949): 618–29.

Chapter 3. Fathering a Maritime Strategy

1. Forrestal to Bieri, 20 Jul 1946, quoted in Millis, *Forrestal Diaries,* p. 184. Forrestal's policy is similar to what is currently termed a Freedom of Navigation (FON) cruise.

2. Conolly, who had been DCNO (Operations) following the OPNAV reorganization of December 1945, was replaced by Sherman early in 1946. Conolly was the Navy's first notable postwar commander in Europe. On 1 November 1947 his command, answerable to the JCS under the Unified Command Plan, was redesignated U.S. Naval Forces, Eastern Atlantic and Mediterranean. Conolly's cumbrous title, CINCNAVEAST-LANTMED, was shortened in May 1948 to CINCNELM.

3. OP-Order 1-46, 1 Apr 1946, Eighth Fleet, Plans File; Command Narrative, 23 Dec 1946, Eighth Fleet, Command File. Emphasis in the original.

4. Arleigh A. Burke, interview with John T. Mason, Jr., 1979, Special Series, 4 vols., 1: 480, USNI Oral History (hereafter Burke Oral History).

5. Forrestal to Bieri, 20 Jul 1946, quoted in Millis, *Forrestal Diaries,* p. 184.

6. Marx Leva, "Barring the Door to the Med," *Proceedings* 113 (Aug

1987): 83–88; letter of W. C. Mott regarding Turner's role in the episode in ibid., 113 (Dec 1987): 110. Turner at the time was the U.S. Navy representative on the United Nations Military Staff Committee.

7. Marx Leva, assistant to Secretary Forrestal, attributes the idea for the *Missouri* mission to Sherman. See Marx Leva, "Secretary of Defense James V. Forrestal in Retrospect: The View Back, after Fifteen Years," MS, pp. 9–11, Command File; Forrestal Diaries, 28 Feb 1946, 4: 900.

8. Burke Oral History, 1: 519. During an earlier visit Forrestal was so informed. See Millis, *Forrestal Diaries,* 183.

9. While American interest and buildup of naval forces in the Mediterranean marked a growing concern with European affairs, the Pacific Fleet remained the stronger fleet until 1948. The Navy's Basic Establishment Plan 1-47 called for a 165-ship Pacific Fleet and a 154-ship Atlantic Fleet, although 8 of 14 large carriers and 3 of 4 battleships were deployed in the Atlantic. BNEPs 1-47 and 1-48, Command File.

10. Memo from the CNO, Résumé of Pincher Planning, 21 Jan 1947, A16-3(5), box 111, Strategic Plans.

11. Memo of 7 June 1946, subj: 6 Jun 1946 OP-30 conference on war planning with OP-03, A16-3(5), box 107, Strategic Plans.

12. Members of the OP-30 staff represented the Navy on the Joint Strategic Plans Committee of the JCS.

13. Commander Carrier Division One, 13 Apr 1946, Operation Frostbite, 1-28 Mar 1946, 3 vols., Report File; Projects, Letters, Memorandums, and Instructions for Operation Nanook, Jun 1946, Command File. Frostbite centered around the operations of *Midway* (CVB-41).

14. Minutes of the first conference, ASW, 17 Jun 1946, ASW Conference series, CNO, Command File.

15. C. H. Waddington, *O.R. in World War 2: Operational Research against the U-boat* (London, 1973), p. 227. Prepared for publication in 1946, Waddington's work was withheld for security reasons.

16. Ibid., pp. 237–38; Charles M. Sternhell and Alan M. Thorndike, *Antisubmarine Warfare in World War II* (Washington, 1946), pp. 143–47. The basic concept behind the Biscay offensive was submarine density: the more submarines transiting an area, the smaller the area; and the more hours spent in flight over the area, the greater the chance of detecting and destroying submarines. If the combination of these factors was right and the offensive capability to detect and sink submarines was present or, conversely, if the means to defend convoys was absent, then offensive measures would be more productive. Soviet submarines would have to transit the narrow area between the Arctic ice pack and the North Cape. Even after the Soviets overran Western Europe, including the Biscay ports of France, they would be forced, as had the Germans, to transit the bay to reach the open Atlantic. See also Keith R. Tidman, *The*

Operations Evaluation Group: A History of Naval Operations Analysis (Annapolis, 1984), pp. 118–22.

17. House Committee on Armed Services, *Sundry Legislation Affecting the Naval and Military Establishments,* 81st Cong., 2d sess., 1950, p. 5952.

18. NSPS 6, "A Study of the Control of the Russian Submarine Menace at Its Source," 19 Jun 1947, updated 21 Aug 1947, box 497; NSPS 7, "A Study of the Control and Protection of Shipping and the Conduct of Anti-Submarine Operations," 29 July 1947, box 498, Strategic Plans.

19. Davis, *Postwar Defense Policy,* pp. 148–49.

20. NSPS 3, "Study of Carrier Attack Force Offensive Capabilities," 7 Mar 1947, box 497, Strategic Plans.

21. The development of the Air Force's B-36 intercontinental bomber was meant to overcome the need for forward bases. The Navy argued that shorter-ranged escort fighters would still need overseas bases while the Air Force believed that B-36 bombers could operate unescorted.

22. OP-30 requested a JANAID (Joint Army-Navy Air Intelligence Division) study of "Russian capabilities of launching air attacks against a U.S. carrier task force 100–200 miles" from Murmansk, Archangel, Southern Kattegat, the Bosporus, Vladivostok, Port Arthur, Sovetskaya Gayan, Nikolaevsk, Paramushiro, Otamari, and Etorfu Shima. The first four were noted as "points particularly pertinent." Memo of 9 Apr 1947 (signed on 11 Apr), A-8, box 111, Strategic Plans.

23. Robert Frank Futrell, *Ideas, Concepts, Doctrine: A History of Basic Thinking in the United States Air Force, 1907–1964* (Maxwell AFB, 1971), pp. 95–134.

24. "Availability of Forces for Emergencies Short of War," 8 Apr 1947, JCS 1763.

25. NSPS 9, "Naval Base Sites in the Mediterranean Area," 16 Aug 1947, box 498, Strategic Plans.

26. David Alan Rosenberg, "The U.S. Navy and the Problem of Oil in a Future War: The Outline of a Strategic Dilemma, 1945–1950," *Naval War College Review* 29 (Summer 1976): 53–64. The American naval presence in the Persian Gulf dates back to 1947 when Navy tankers began loading fuel oil at Ras Tanura, Saudi Arabia. Naval forces operated directly under CINCNELM until the Persian Gulf Area Command was established in 1949. Later in the year the command's name was changed to Middle East Force. See Middle East Force, Command History, 1 Jan 1949–31 Dec 1958; CINCNELM, Command Report, 1 Jul 1948–30 Jul 1949, Command File.

27. CINCPAC, Joint Staff Study Triagonal, 31 Oct 1947, Plans File.

28. For a review of Pacific plans, see Roger Dingman, "Strategic Planning and the Policy Process: American Plans for War in East Asia, 1945–1950," *Naval War College Review* 32 (Nov–Dec 1979): 4–21.

29. "Strategic Estimate and Deployment in the Pacific," 2 Apr 1947, p. 286, JCS 1259/36, declared that for "the proximate future, United States military strategy in the Pacific should be offensive-defensive in nature, should recognize that the area is of operational importance secondary to the European Mediterranean area."

30. Joint Staff Study Triagonal, 31 Oct 1947, CINCPAC, Plans File. Denfeld was also CINCPACFLT.

31. Top Secret presentations to the President, Senate, and House, no. 26, box 8, Sherman Papers. See also "Résumé of Pincher Planning," Memorandum for the CNO, 21 Jan 1947, A 16-3, box 111, Strategic Plans.

32. Sherman, Presentation to the President's Advisory Committee on the Merchant Marine, 29 Apr 1947, Command File.

33. The Navy's overseas deployments were, of course, widely publicized, especially those in the Mediterranean. Its peacetime missions of supporting allies and deterring war were openly discussed. But key elements of American plans for war with the Soviet Union, such as the "swing" strategy that would shift the bulk of the Pacific Fleet to the Atlantic and the planned evacuation of U.S. ground forces from continental Europe, were not openly discussed. On 10 May 1952, the French newspaper *Le Monde* printed a bogus, but relatively accurate, study that wrote off Western Europe in the event of a Soviet offensive. The United States vehemently denied the authenticity of the report, allegedly authored by Admiral William M. Fechteler, CNO. See *Le Monde* article file, box 6, 1952, 00 File.

34. The Maritime Strategy briefings by the Navy in the 1980s closely resemble Sherman's in their use of visual aids to illustrate what a Soviet force might accomplish in the early stages of a Soviet-American battle of the Atlantic. House Seapower and Strategic and Critical Materials Subcommittee of the Committee on Armed Services, *The 600-Ship Navy and the Maritime Strategy,* 99th Cong., 1st sess., 1985, pp. 12–115.

35. The Air Force's focus on nuclear strategic bombing and the absence of large Army formations overseas meant that the Navy would bear the initial conventional burden of slowing any Soviet advance while it kept open the SLOCs to those forward bases from which any subsequent counteroffensive would be launched.

36. Top Secret presentations to the President, Senate, and House, no. 26, box 8, Sherman Papers.

37. According to Sherman, the Soviet Navy consisted of "four battleships, eleven cruisers, fifty-eight destroyers, forty-five destroyer escorts . . . and the several hundred amphibious, mine, patrol, and auxiliary types."

38. Desmond Wettern, *The Decline of British Seapower* (London, 1982),

pp. 392–93; International Institute for Strategic Studies, *The Military Balance, 1986–1987* (London, 1986), pp. 22, 39; BNEP 1-48, Command File.

39. "Study of Fundamentals for the Development of Naval Requirements," encl A to CNO ltr of 11 Mar 1947, A 16-3, box 110, Strategic Plans. A mobilization study prepared under Sherman's guidance late in 1946 was reissued with minor modifications and extended to 1952. "Strategic Aspects upon which to base Navy Mobilization Requirements," 30 Oct 1946, encl to DCNO(Operations) ltr, 1 Nov 1946, A 16-3, box 497, Strategic Plans. The revised version of the report, dated 17 Jan 1949, is attached to an OP-30 memo of that date in the same folder.

Chapter 4. A Strategy Challenged

1. Denfeld to Sullivan, 5 May 1948, discusses Admiral Conolly's recommendations and reasons for changing the name of U.S. Naval Forces, Mediterranean to Sixth Task Fleet. File 5, box 2, 00 File.

2. Burke attributes the key role to Radford, but Radford credits Sherman. See Burke Oral History, 1: 82, and Arthur W. Radford, *From Pearl Harbor to Vietnam: The Memoirs of Admiral Arthur W. Radford,* Stephen Jurika, Jr., ed. (Stanford, CA, 1980), p. 98. Admiral J. J. "Jocko" Clark attributed the agreement to Sherman. See J. J. Clark and Clark G. Reynolds, *Carrier Admiral* (New York, 1967), p. 249; and Futrell, *Ideas, Concepts, Doctrine,* pp. 96–97.

3. Jurika, ed., *Pearl Harbor to Vietnam,* p. 101.

4. Ibid., p. 101. Jurika, in his edited version of Radford's memoirs, deleted two pages in which Radford discussed the personal differences between Nimitz and himself over the responsibility for aviation assignments. See Arthur W. Radford, MS, pp. 493–95, Command File. Nimitz had considered Radford's discussion of his opposition to the unification compromise with *New York Times* correspondent Hanson W. Baldwin a security breach. Nimitz to Radford, and Radford to Nimitz, 28 Jan 1947, no. 5, Series I, DCNO (Air).

5. Just as Radford had replaced Mitscher early in 1946 as DCNO (Air), Sherman had replaced Conolly as DCNO (Operations).

6. Clark G. Reynolds, "Forrest Percival Sherman," in Robert William Love, Jr., ed., *The Chiefs of Naval Operations* (Annapolis, 1980), p. 211.

7. Others, notably Vice Admirals Marc Mitscher, Commander Third Fleet, and John H. Towers, former Chief of Staff under Nimitz, stood to the side. Admiral Robert B. Carney commented: "Sherman was a hell of a smart savvy bird, no two ways about it. But he was able to maneuver himself into a position which excluded Jack Towers, the Chief of Staff." Asked if Sherman was the dominant figure in OPNAV under Nimitz, Carney replied: "Oh, yes, yes. Well, all I have to do is tell you to take a

look at that picture of the surrender. That tells you the whole story. He had Admiral Nimitz in his pocket. That sounds much more of a slur than I intended. What I meant was that Admiral Nimitz was very much convinced of his superior analytic abilities." Carney, interview with author, 2 Jul 1987, Naval Historical Center (NHC), Washington, DC (hereafter Carney Interview). Sherman's flag secretary, Rear Admiral Ira H. Nunn, also referred to the surrender picture. Nunn, interview with author, 8 Jul 1987, NHC. Sherman also rode with Admiral Nimitz during the Washington, DC, victory parade.

8. "Jocko" Clark saw the Navy divided into two "camps." The first included Nimitz, Ramsey, and Sherman; and the second, Radford, Clark, and the aviation community that supported them. Clark and Reynolds, *Carrier Admiral,* pp. 249–50. Carney also favored a three department defense organization that included an independent Air Force. Carney to Ramsey and Nimitz, 25 Nov 1946, file 31, box 2, 1942–1947, 00 File.

9. During the war Sherman commanded the carrier *Wasp,* sunk in September 1942. After the war he briefly commanded Carrier Division One.

10. Clark and Reynolds, *Carrier Admiral,* pp. 253, 393.

11. Ramsey to Sherman, 2 Nov 1949, box 3, Sherman Papers.

12. Sherman to Denfeld, 20 Jan 1948, box 6, Denfeld Papers.

13. Charles D. Griffin, interview with John T. Mason, Jr., 1973, 2 vols, 1: 192, USNI Oral History.

14. Ruthven E. Libby, interview with Paul Stillwell, 1984, pp. 167–68, USNI Oral History.

15. Ibid., p. 168; and Griffin Oral History, 2: 197.

16. Carney Interview, 2 Jul 1987.

17. U.S. Navy Department, *Manual for the Office of the Chief of Naval Operations* (hereafter *OCNO Manual*) (Washington, Nov 1945), E. B. Potter's, *Nimitz* (Annapolis, 1976), p. 428, states that Nimitz was tired after his Pacific victories. Admiral Burke points out that after the war "everybody was tired." Arleigh A. Burke, interview with author, 9 Jul 1987, NHC (hereafter Burke Interview). Admiral Carney felt that "Nimitz came in there to complete the record as Chief of Naval Operations." Carney Interview, 2 Jul 1987. At Second Fleet headquarters, both Mitscher and Burke viewed DCNOs Radford (Air), Sherman (Operations), and Carney (Logistics) as the key players in the OPNAV hierarchy. Burke Oral History, 4: 523; Burke Interview, 9 Jul 1987.

18. In the November 1945 manual, the VCNO was allotted eight lines of text; in the 1948 manual twenty-three, more than the CNO himself. *OCNO Manual* (Washington, Aug 1948), pp. 1–2; ibid. (Nov 1945), pp. 1–2.

19. Sherman retained the language in his 1950 revision of the manual. *OCNO Manual* (Washington, Nov 1950), p. 1.

20. Radford and Carney, who handled the budget and logistics, dominated OPNAV. Under Nimitz, Carney had left strategic matters to Sherman. Carney Interview, 2 Jul 1987. See also Carney to Nimitz, 2 Dec 1946, file 31, box 2, 1942–1947, 00 File. Carney did not see the Navy conducting offensive operations in the Pacific. He envisioned reducing facilities at Pearl Harbor and using Truk as a major fleet base. Although Truk was "somewhat further removed from any likely scene of operations," Carney noted that "from the passive defense standpoint this may be an asset rather than a liability." When Sherman saw the memo he noted in the margin that the Pearl Harbor recommendation was "questionable," that Truk was "an anchorage rather than a well developed shore base," and that Carney's "'assumptions'" were "not the best available."

21. Draft paper 2, Feb 1948, p. 7, A1/EM-3/4-2, CNO S&C, OP-23.

22. Draft 1, Feb 1948, p. 15, ibid.

23. Presentation before the House Appropriations Naval Subcommittee, 5 Feb 1948, Chronological file, CNO, Command File. The presentation, nevertheless, reflected the work of Sherman and his staff planners, especially Anderson who had worked for the former OP-03. Several charts used in the February 1948 briefing were either similar or identical to ones used by Sherman in April and October 1947. Sherman, Presentation to the President's Advisory Committee on the Merchant Marine, 29 Apr 1947, Command File; Presentation before the Joint Congressional Air Policy board, 2 Oct 1947, Sherman, Biographical Files. Compare the charts Sherman described in his 29 April 1947 presentation (pp. 10–20) and the U.S. Lifelines chart used on 2 October 1947 (after p. 11) with the charts presented in February 1948. The lifeline charts are identical.

24. "Naval Air Power," Presentation before the Committee on the National Security Organization of the Commission on Organization of the Executive Branch of the Government by John Nicholas Brown, Assistant Secretary of the Navy for Air and Vice Admiral Arthur W. Radford, pp. 4, 20, A21/1 Policy, S&C, OP-23.

25. Thackrey, the author of Nimitz's "Valedictory," was head of SCOROR's successor, the Unification Committee (UNICOM).

26. Thackrey to Radford, 3 Sep 1948, A21/1 Policy, S&C, OP-23.

27. Forrestal to Charles Gurney, 2 Apr 1948, no. 9, Series I, DCNO (Air).

28. BNEPs 1-48 and 1-49, Command File.

29. Ibid.

30. Price to Carl Spaatz, 20 Apr 1948, no. 9, Series I, DCNO (Air).

31. Price to Denfeld, 28 Sep 1948, no. 9, Series I, DCNO (Air).

32. Ibid.

33. Thackrey noted the problem in a memo written after reading

Naval Air Power. Thackrey to Pihl, 19 Oct 1948, A21/1 Policy, S&C, OP-23.

34. Frank Futrell concludes that the Air Force's concentration on strategic nuclear attack ultimately proved counterproductive:

> Lest anyone miss it, my overall conclusion is going to be that the revolutionary strategic power enthusiasts—who focused on developing flight for independent military actions—overlooked a real worth of air activity in a synergy of total military power, as a cooperative permitter, expeditor, and force multiplier in a total scenario of war. Acceptance of a bombs-on-target concept of air power strapped the Air Force into a lone wolf configuration poorly prepared for the requirements of war and confrontation in the years following the Cuban missile crisis of 1962. Futrell, "The Influence of the Air Power Concept on Air Force Planning, 1945–1962," in Harry R. Borowski, ed., *Military Planning in the Twentieth Century: Proceedings of the Eleventh Military History Symposium* (Washington, 1986), p. 253.

35. Norman Friedman, *U.S. Aircraft Carriers: An Illustrated Design History* (Annapolis, 1983), pp. 239–53.

36. Norman to Sherman, 15 Apr 1949, box 3, Sherman Papers.

37. Ibid.

38. Radford believed that Secretary of Defense Johnson was eager to get the Navy's VCNO out of Washington. See Jurika, ed., *From Pearl Harbor to Vietnam,* pp. 148–49.

39. Ibid., p. 143.

40. BNEP 1-50 (Nov 1949), Command File. Sherman issued a revised BNEP in February 1950. The November 1949 plan reduced the number of ships in the Pacific Fleet from 128 to 96. At the same time the Atlantic Fleet grew from 142 to 183 ships and gained strength in every combatant category except antiaircraft cruisers.

41. Harry R. Borowski, *A Hollow Threat: Strategic Air Power and Containment before Korea* (Westport and London, 1982).

42. Richard Conolly, interview with Donald F. Shaughnessy, 1960, p. 392, Columbia University Oral History Project, New York, NY (hereafter Conolly Oral History). Conolly was aware that he was to be the next CNO. Radford had been relieved as VCNO and sent to Hawaii as CINCPACFLT.

43. Ibid., p. 393.

44. Ibid., p. 394.

45. Carney, too, had serious reservations. "Raddy and I, because we're classmates, we were tangling horns the whole time. And his position, quite frankly, was to get all the aviators in the top positions, and I wasn't about to buy that. I felt there had to be far more balance than that.

I wasn't anti-aviation, but I was anti-aviation empire." Carney Interview, 2 Jul 1987. See also Carney to Ramsey and Nimitz, 25 Nov 1946, file 31, box 2, 1942–1947, 00 File. Carney believed it possible that technical changes had brought naval aviation "to the end of the road." Burke also felt that Radford "overemphasized naval aviation." Burke Interview, 9 Jul 1987.

46. Oct 1949, Press Releases.

47. Radford received hesitant support from his superior at the last minute. Denfeld drafted his statement the day before he was scheduled to testify. In a second major section of the testimony, entitled "A Balanced Navy," Denfeld reiterated several themes developed over the years: the ASW mission, the importance of attacking submarines at their bases, SLOC defense, and amphibious warfare. Statement before the B-36 Committee, box 9, Denfeld Papers; Coletta, *The Navy and Defense Unification,* pp. 189–90; Carney Interview, 2 Jul 1987.

48. The Pacific command in the late 1940s was not the plum it had been before or during the Second World War, nor would become after 1950. The peacetime strength of the fleet was being reduced each year. In wartime the Pacific Fleet's striking power was destined for the Persian Gulf and the Eastern Atlantic. There were even rumors of downgrading the CINCPAC/CINCPACFLT command post from four to three stars. See Jurika, ed., *From Pearl Harbor to Vietnam,* pp. 144, 148.

49. Herbert H. Anderson, interview with author, 22 Jul 1987, NHC.

50. Standby Statements B-36 Hearings, Forrest Sherman, D-1, OP-23.

51. Conolly Oral History, p. 405.

52. According to Conolly, Sherman confided his expectations to Mrs. Conolly. Ibid., p. 406.

53. Secretary of the Navy Matthews all but promised Conolly that he would succeed Denfeld as CNO if he avoided a direct attack on the administration. Conolly felt the suggestion was not far removed from a bribe, and out of conviction refused to adopt the Denfeld-Radford tactics of direct attacks against unification and the B-36. In his testimony he stressed the need for a strong, balanced Navy. But Carl Vinson's hard questioning forced Conolly into Radford's corner. Vinson had been working closely with Radford whom he had recalled from the Pacific earlier in the year. Conolly, Oral History, p. 398; Vinson to Matthews, 6 Aug 1949; Matthews to Vinson, 8 Aug 1949; Kimball to Vinson, 16 Aug 1949; Admiral Radford, C-10, B-36 Hearing Papers, OP-23. Conolly ended his career as head of the Naval War College.

54. Potter, *Nimitz,* pp. 447–48. At the White House, George Elsey and Clark Clifford noted Sherman's work on unification. Elsey to Sherman, 3 Nov 1949; and Clifford to Sherman, 7 Nov 1949, box 1, Sherman Papers.

Chapter 5. A Strategy Reasserted

1. Anderson Interview, 22 Jul 1987.

2. Of the officers senior to Sherman on the list, Admirals Kincaid (61), Conolly (57), and Blandy (59) testified during the B-36 hearings, as had Vice Admiral Radford. Vice Admirals George D. Murray (60), Harry Hill (59), John L. Hall, Jr. (58), and Oscar C. Badger (59) had not testified but were passed over. Although Radford and Sherman, both 53, had been promoted to rear admiral on the same day—28 December 1945—Radford was senior because he graduated earlier from the Naval Academy. Of the eight men besides Sherman eligible for appointment, only Conolly and Radford probably had the qualifications to serve as CNO. Radford, at least, had made a personal decision based on his convictions. He went on to serve as Chairman of the JCS. Conolly, who personally disagreed with Radford's approach, deserves the sympathy of the historian.

3. Carney Interview, 2 Jul 1987.

4. Towers to Sherman, 2 Nov 1949, box 4, Sherman Papers.

5. Sherman to Towers, 11 Nov 1949, box 4, Sherman Papers. At Truman's press conference on 27 October 1949, following the announcement of Denfeld's relief as CNO, a reporter asked the President: "Is Admiral Sherman replacing him?" Truman responded, "I can't answer that question." U.S. President, *Public Papers of the President of the United States: Harry S Truman,* 8 vols. (Washington, 1961–1966), 5: 531.

6. Read to Sherman, 2 Nov 1949; Ramsey to Sherman, 2 Nov 1949, box 3, Sherman Papers. Ramsey wrote: "No one knows better than I do that this event has been in the making over a long period of years."

7. Carney Interview, 2 Jul 1987. Burke remarked: "He [Sherman] was good in all parts and he knew it, and he knew a great deal of the responsibility of the future would rest on his head. So he better be prepared for it." Burke Interview, 9 Jul 1987.

8. Sherman to Denfeld, 8 Apr 1948, box 6, Denfeld Papers. Conolly noted in his oral history, "I know he [Sherman] was amazed when he got the call." Conolly Oral History, p. 406.

9. Sherman to Towers, 11 Nov 1949, box 4, Sherman Papers. Author's emphasis.

10. William M. Fechteler, interview with John T. Mason, Jr., 1962, p. 86, Columbia University Oral History Project; Nunn Interview, 8 Jul 1987.

11. Eisenhower to Edward Everett Hazelett, Jr., 24 Feb 1950, Alfred D. Chandler and Louis Galambos, eds., *The Papers of Dwight David Eisenhower,* 11 vols. (Baltimore and London, 1970–1984), 11: 988–94.

12. Steven L. Rearden, *History of the Office of the Secretary of Defense,* vol. 1, *The Formative Years, 1947–1950* (Washington, 1984), p. 420n.

13. Omar N. Bradley and Clay Blair, *A General's Life* (New York, 1983), pp. 513, 534, 647. George C. Marshall also thought highly of Sherman and corresponded with him during the war when the Army had stabled the latter's horse at Fort Myer. See Forrest C. Pogue, *George C. Marshall: Statesman, 1945–1949* (New York, 1987), p. 440.

14. See *Time,* 13 Mar 1950. Sherman wrote on his copy of the article that the story was inaccurate: "I usually wear flannels and an odd coat & we are very informal at home." The *Time* photo of the admiral and Mrs. Sherman in formal wear was taken "prior to dining with the President and the Shah." Sherman, Biographical Files.

15. See the following Sherman contributions in *Proceedings:* "Comment and Discussion," 60 (Apr 1934): 550–51; "The British Occupation of Guantanamo Bay," 57 (Apr 1931): 509–512; "Air Operations in Palestine," 53 (Jul 1927): 787–92; and reviews of the Byng Papers in 57 (May 1931): 702–703; (Oct 1931): 1432–33; and 59 (Apr 1933): 586–87.

16. Sherman, "Air Warfare," ibid. 52 (Jan 1926): 70–71.

17. Sherman, "Air Tactics and Strategy," ibid. 52 (May 1926): 858.

18. Sherman, "Review of Economy and Naval Security," ibid. 58 (Jun 1932): 912–13.

19. Sherman's Standby Statement, D-1, OP-23.

20. *Lucky Bag,* 1918, p. 194.

21. Burke Oral History, 1: 512.

22. In an earlier letter Hazelett wrote that Sherman had a reputation as "an intellectual snob" and would "never have the wholehearted support of his own service." See *Eisenhower Papers,* 10: 835n; 11: 864n, 994n.

23. Conolly Oral History, p. 405.

24. Burke Oral History, 1: 511–12.

25. See Sherman's official Navy biography in box 7, Sherman Papers; and *Time,* 13 Mar 1950, p. 22.

26. Carney commented that Sherman had avoided being "tar brushed" during the B-36 hearings "and there was one other who managed to go on leave for two or three weeks [Admiral Fechteler] and avoid all the hurrah." Carney Interview, 2 Jul 1987. Another noted aviator who did not testify was "Jocko" Clark.

27. Radford MS, pp. 833–35.

28. Byrd to Sherman, 10 Apr 1950, quotes a Radford to Byrd letter of 6 Mar 1950. Box 1, Sherman Papers.

29. An OP-03 committee headed by Rear Admiral Frederick W. McMahon also completed a study on carrier operations in the Mediterranean that reiterated the 1946–1947 call for aggressive operations. Vice Admiral Struble, DCNO (Operations), considered the differences between the McMahon and CINCNELM studies "largely attributable to differences of interpretation of the language used to express the conclu-

sions of the CincNelm Study. No formal approval or disapproval of either Study is contemplated." Struble to Radford, 7 Mar 1949, A4-3, box 1, 1949, 00 File.

30. Tab A. Conclusions and Recommendations, Carrier Task Group Operations in the Mediterranean: a CINCNELM Staff Study, no. 79, box 481, Strategic Plans. Emphasis in the original.

31. Staff planners, some of whom had worked under Sherman the year before, thought the study represented a misuse of carrier offensive potential by putting the cart, air-to-air defense, before the horse, air-to-ground attacks. The study may have represented a compromise between an aggressive Sherman and a cautious Conolly. According to Carney, Sherman and Conolly were "at swordpoints all the time." Carney Interview, 2 Jul 1987. The mixture of caution and aggressiveness is evident in the sketch plans for strikes via Turkish bases against Black Sea ports. Carney's concept of carrier operations in the Mediterranean retains the note of sensible caution evident in the CINCNELM study: "come into Gibraltar and go as far east as you can, but don't be a damned fool." Carney Interview, 2 Jul 1987.

32. Brightness, 23 Dec 1948, CINCPACFLT, Plans File.

33. National Security Organization, "National Security and Navy Contributions Thereto for the Next Ten Years," A General Board Study, encl D, p. 52, A1/2, OP-23; David A. Rosenberg, *Historical Perspectives in Long-Range Planning in the Navy* (Washington, 1980), pp. 20–21.

34. See Sherman's 20 March 1950 testimony, Senate Subcommittee of the Committee on Appropriations, *Department of Defense Appropriations for 1953,* 81st Cong., 2d sess., 1950, p. 200.

35. David Alan Rosenberg, "American Postwar Air Doctrine and Organization: The Navy Experience," in Hurley and Ehrhart, *Air Power and Warfare,* pp. 261–63.

36. CNO to list, 20 May 1949, attached with the "Study of U.S.S.R. Plan of Submarine Warfare Against U.S.-U.K." to COMSUBPAC to CNO, 4 Aug 1949, Chronological file, SUBPAC, Command File.

37. "Soviet Capabilitied [*sic*] in Undersea Warfare in 1950 and in 1955," in the Report of the Fourth Anti-Submarine Conference, 28 Nov 1949, Washington, DC, pp. 11–27, ASW Conference series, CNO, Command File.

38. "Study of Undersea Warfare," 22 Apr 1950, p. 5, Studies, Command File. The study found the 1950 Soviet submarine fleet "less formidable than the German U-Boat fleet of World War II, being mostly composed of submarines inferior to the standard German types." See also Rosenberg, "The Navy Experience," p. 275n.

39. "Study of Undersea Warfare," p. 2.

40. Ibid., p. 6. The April 1950 report reaffirmed the need for fast carrier task forces to bomb and mine Soviet bases and their approaches to prevent submarines from entering the Atlantic or the Pacific.

41. CNO to list, OPNAV Presentation to Weapons Systems Evaluation Group on fleet air defense as applied to the carrier task force, 7 Sep 1950, DOD, Command File.

42. JCS 2131/1, 28 Feb 1952. The detailed enclosures remain classified. As DCNO, Sherman had advocated a four-carrier task group, the optimum number based on the Navy's Pacific experience. See also Mitscher to Forrestal, 24 Sep 1945, no. 4, Series I, DCNO (Air).

43. The study expected operational efficiency in the Barents Sea to be reduced by about 40 percent. The Navy criticized the study for being too sanguine and ignoring the primary threat to carrier task force operations—Soviet submarines.

44. Norman Friedman, *U.S. Destroyers* (Annapolis, 1982), pp. 245–47.

45. Report of the Fourth Anti-Submarine Conference, 28 Nov 1949, p. 160, ASW Conference series, CNO, Command File. Congress, lest there be any doubt, sought assurances from Sherman himself. See Sherman's 27 April 1950 testimony in House Committee on Armed Services, *Sundry Legislation Affecting the Naval and Military Establishments,* 81st Cong., 2d sess., 1950, p. 5952.

46. A CINCPACFLT staff study concluded that submarines would be able to conduct more traditional antishipping operations in the Pacific than in European waters.

> Submarines of the Pacific Fleet can also give offensive support to CinCFE and CinCAL by conducting offensive torpedo patrols. In the *Far East* the Soviets have, in addition to a fleet of 101 submarines, 32 major combatants and approximately 1,000,000 tons of tankers and other vital shipping, which will undoubtedly be augmented through seizure of shipping of other nations. In view of the limited rail capacity of *Eastern Russia,* the tankers and merchant shipping are of vital importance to the *Soviet* war-making effort in the *Far East.* Destruction of these tankers and shipping are, therefore, one of the major targets for our submarines. COMSUBPAC to CNO, 23 Nov 1948, enclosing COMSUBPAC to CINCPACFLT, 19 Nov 1948, covering staff study "Initial Operations of Pacific Fleet Submarines in the Event of a General Emergency," pp. 11–12, Chronological file, SUBPAC, Command File.

Submarine lifeguarding supported carrier task force and land-based air operations by recovering downed aviators.

47. Minutes, Submarine Conference Steering Group, 21 Nov 1949, p. 2, Submarine Warfare Conference series, CNO, Command File.

48. For a good view of the postwar doldrums faced by submariners after their victory see Clay Blair, Jr., *Silent Victory: The U.S. Submarine War against Japan* (Philadelphia and New York, 1975), pp. 877–85.

49. Biographical Files.

50. Roy S. Benson address at the Fourth Anti-Submarine Conference, 28 Nov–2 Dec 1949, "Current Consensus on Anti-Submarine Situation in Submarine Development Group Two," p. 132, ASW Conference series, CNO, Command File.

51. Ibid., p. 135; CO, *Cochino* to COMSUBLANT, 8 Sep 1949, Submarine Reports; and COMSUBLANT to CNO, 14 Sep 1949, enclosing report of Submarine Development Group Two, 22 Jul 1949, Chronological file, SUBLANT, Command File. As the result of a battery room fire, *Cochino* sank the following day at latitude 71° 45' north, longitude 24° 20' east.

52. Norman Polmar and Thomas B. Allen, *Rickover* (New York, 1982), pp. 145–48. Sherman pushed the idea of a nuclear-powered aircraft carrier in 1950, when Captain Hyman Rickover, the major proponent of nuclear propulsion, considered the moment inopportune. Rickover soon embraced the idea, but with Sherman's death in 1951 the concept was shelved. Ibid., pp. 251–52. See also Richard G. Hewlett and Francis Duncan, *Nuclear Navy, 1946–1962* (Chicago and London, 1974), pp. 196–97.

53. JCS 1844/46, 8 Dec 1949; JCS 2143/1, 5 Oct 1950.

54. JCS 1920/5. While the language describing the carrier tasks conflicted with Radford's position, it paralleled earlier Navy studies such as NSPS 3, completed in early 1947 under Sherman.

55. For a discussion of the Navy's response to JCS plans during Denfeld's tenure see Kenneth W. Condit, *The History of the Joint Chiefs of Staff: The Joint Chiefs of Staff and National Policy,* vol. 2, *1947–1949* (Washington, 1978), pp. 277–87.

56. C. W. Lord, Navy Presentation of Current Emergency War Plan, 9 Nov 1949, JCS 1844/46.

57. Greece and Turkey accepted invitations to take part in defense planning in the Mediterranean in October 1950. Both nations joined NATO on 18 February 1952. NATO Information Service, *NATO Facts and Figures* (Brussels, Belgium, 1971), pp. 227, 229.

58. Sherman to JCS, 7 Dec 1949, JCS 1944/46. Two days later Radford forwarded a study to Sherman that concluded "the overall U.S. naval strength available in the Pacific on D-day in accordance with current directives, inactivation schedules and redeployment commitments is inadequate to perform the naval missions assigned." Radford to Sherman, 9 Dec 1949, enclosing CINCPACFLT Revised Staff Study of PACFLT Missions and Force Requirements, A4-3, box 1, 1949, 00 File. See also

Sherman's testimony, 20 Feb 1950, House Subcommittee of the Committee on Appropriations, *Department of the Navy,* 81st Cong., 2d sess., 1950, pt. 4, pp. 1744, 1754. The JCS's concession that allowed Sherman to maintain a fleet of seven carriers, rather than six, enabled the Navy to maintain at least one carrier in the Western Pacific.

59. Had he lived, Sherman would have served until the fall of 1953 as CNO and possibly would have succeeded Bradley as Chairman of the JCS when the latter retired in early 1953. A relatively young Sherman then would have influenced American strategy for another four years. Other factors contributed to the Navy's rising fortunes: the public stand taken by senior naval officers during the B-36 hearings, the outbreak of war in Korea, and the changing national mood. Radford MS, p. 833; Jurika, ed., *Pearl Harbor to Vietnam,* p. 220. See especially Davis, *The Admirals Lobby,* p. 321n. Davis attributes the upturn in the Navy's fortunes to the Truman administration's search for a military method to pressure the Chinese Communists. Of the service chiefs consulted, only Sherman offered a workable proposal, but one that required an increase of naval forces. Pressure was already building to reverse the downturn in military spending and national preparedness, pressure that would culminate in NSC 68, presented to Truman on 14 April 1950. See U.S. Department of State, *Foreign Relations of the United States, 1950,* vol. 1, *National Security Affairs: Foreign Economic Policy,* S. Everett Gleason and Frederick Aandahl, eds. (Washington, 1977), pp. 234–92. NSC 68 noted:

> The history of war also indicates that a favorable decision can only be achieved through offensive action. Even a defensive strategy, if it is to be successful, calls not only for defensive forces to hold vital positions while mobilizing and preparing for the offensive, but also for offensive forces to attack the enemy and keep him off balance. Ibid., pp. 282–83.

Sherman also purposefully played down the Navy's capabilities and interest in a strategic warfare campaign. Vice Admiral J. H. Cassady, DCNO (Air), noted in a memo to Sherman:

> You will remember that at one time we declared for attack aircraft with a combat radius of 1700 miles. It was emphasized that such a radius would permit carrier-based aircraft to attack any target any place in the world. This was immediately seized upon as an indication of our intention to go into the strategic bombing business. I feel that a 1700 mile figure should be discarded and we should go out for a combat radius of something in the neighborhood of 1300–1400 miles (if we ever get the flush-decker we could increase combat radius as available). Cassady to Sherman, 12 May 1950, no. 11, Series I, DCNO (Air).

60. See Sherman's 27 April 1950 testimony in House Committee on Armed Services, *Sundry Legislation Affecting the Naval and Military Establishments,* 81st Cong., 2d sess., 1950, pp. 5952–53.

61. *U.S. News and World Report,* 23 Feb 1951, pp. 33–35.

62. See Sherman's 27 April 1950 testimony in House Committee on Armed Services, *Sundry Legislation Affecting the Naval and Military Establishments,* 81st Cong., 2d sess., 1950, pp. 5960–62.

63. Friedman, *U.S. Aircraft Carriers,* pp. 255–57.

64. JCS 1844/98, the Navy's force tabs revised.

65. Anderson Interview, 22 Jul 1987. As CNO, Sherman killed a Navy Department study on the break up of the office of the DCNO (Air). Sherman to Senior Member, Navy Department Management Survey Board, Sub-Board One, 13 Apr 1950, no. 11, Series I, DCNO (Air).

66. Carney Interview, 2 Jul 1987.

Chapter 6. A Strategy Lost

1. Following Sherman's death, the Truman administration began its fourth search in seven years for a Chief of Naval Operations. The Air Force between 1946 and 1953, by comparison, had two Chiefs of Staff, Generals Carl A. Spaatz and Hoyt S. Vandenberg; and the Army, three Chiefs of Staff, Generals Eisenhower, Bradley, and J. Lawton Collins. Eisenhower and Bradley, of course, remained on the JCS as chairman between 1949 and 1953.

2. Bradley and Blair, *A General's Life,* p. 647.

3. Ibid., p. 659. Despite his stand during the B-36 hearings, Radford was chosen as chairman.

4. ACNO (Underseas Warfare) to Director, Strategic Plans, 25 Sep 1952, enclosing Annex B, Navy Strategic Plan Flotilla, Concept of Operations, A4-3(1), box 273, Strategic Plans. Flotilla was the new codename for Endless.

5. CNO to JCS (Original by A. A. Burke), 28 Nov 1952, A4-3(1), box 273, Strategic Plans. Other Navy plans and studies reiterated the same points. A contingency plan for war with China advocated the neutralization of airfields, submarine and naval bases, and communications centers, and recommended amphibious raids in conjunction with carrier task force operations. A report prepared for the Secretary of Defense listed three primary missions for the Navy—SLOC defense, ground support of NATO, and denial to the Soviets of the Baltic, Norwegian, Aegean, eastern Mediterranean, and Western Pacific. Further, it called for forward offensive carrier operations against Soviet bases. "Navy plan to determine maximum capability to fight a war with Communist China," c. 2/4/52, folder 2; SECNAV to SECDEF, Status of United States

Programs for National Security as of June 30, 1953, 30 Jul 1953, folder 1, A16-1, Top Secret Books, box 5, 1953, 00 File. The report recommended "destroying naval bases and associated units, destroying aircraft on the ground and their operating facilities, destroying enemy naval surface units and shipping at sea, and of establishing local air superiority by destroying enemy aircraft both airborne and at their bases."

6. See Fechteler's 16 June 1952 testimony in Senate Subcommittee of the Committee on Appropriations, *Department of Defense Appropriations for 1953*, 82d Cong., 2d sess., 1952, pp. 1030, 1037, 1047, 1051.

7. Richard A. Best, Jr., *"Cooperation of Like-Minded Peoples": British Influences on American Security Policy, 1945–1949* (New York, Westport and London, 1986), pp. 89–90; Condit, *History of the JCS*, vol. 2, *1947–1949*, pp. 280, 289; Joel J. Sokolsky, "Seapower in the Nuclear Age: NATO as a Maritime Alliance" (Ph.D. diss., Harvard University, 1986), pp. 45–46.

8. Lord Ismay, *NATO: The First Five Years, 1949–1954*, 2d ed. (Utrecht, 1956), pp. 24, 74–75; NAORPG Papers, 9 Nov 1949, Appendix A, p. 4, box 8, 1949, 00 File. The report is initialled by Sherman. The minutes of the first meeting make clear Anglo-American offensive intentions.

9. Memo from the Sea Air Warfare Committee, enclosing the paper Fighter Defense of Convoys, 31 Mar 1951, A19, box 265, Strategic Plans.

10. Quoted in Nigel Hamilton, *Monty: Final Years of the Field-Marshal, 1944–1976* (New York, 1986), pp. 832–35.

11. OP-33 to CNO, 8 Sep 1952, information concerning NATO exercise MAINBRACE, A5, box 1, 1952, 00 File.

12. Burke to list, Strategic Planning for the Defeat of the USSR, 18 Apr 1953, enclosing "Advantages and Disadvantages of Two Courses of Action to Defeat the USSR," A1, box 279, Strategic Plans.

13. Burke to list, 17 Oct 1953, enclosing Burke to DCNO (Operations), 24 Apr 1953, subj: Lack of planning data for naval operations in the Barents Sea, A1, box 279, Strategic Plans.

14. Burke to list, 13 Oct 1953, enclosing a study of attack carrier force levels, A4, box 280, Strategic Plans. Nevertheless, the Mediterranean remained a critically important theater in Navy plans.

15. For the Navy and Marine Corps force levels for 1949 and 1952 see Condit, *History of the JCS*, vol. 2, *1947–1949*, p. 553; and Robert J. Watson, *History of the JCS*, vol. 5, *1953–1954* (Washington: 1986), p. 82.

16. See above, p. 30.

17. The fault was mostly Sherman's. He had delivered many well-received presentations on naval strategy and recognized the value of publicity, but he also was concerned with security. As DCNO he had tried to muzzle OPNAV when Hanson W. Baldwin, a Naval Academy graduate and military editor of the *New York Times,* began work on an

article on the impact of new technology. Forrestal had approved the project, believing it in the best interest of the Navy, and supported Baldwin in the dispute. Baldwin considered Sherman "part of the silent Navy," a man "terse, sometimes a little acerbic, sardonic . . . I may be quite unfair on saying he was a manipulator. But he handled power like that." Hanson W. Baldwin, interview with John T. Mason, Jr., 1976, 2 vols., 2: 481–84, USNI Oral History, Baldwin remembered Sherman being CNO at the time of the incident, but by then Forrestal was dead. The affair must have occurred in 1946 or early 1947 when Sherman was DCNO and Forrestal, still SECNAV. Baldwin's memory lapse may also indicate his sense of Sherman being the dominant force in OPNAV.

18. John B. Hattendorf, B. Mitchell Simpson III, and John R. Wadleigh, *Sailors and Scholars: The Centennial History of the U.S. Naval War College* (Newport, RI, 1984), p. 201.

19. Ibid.

20. J. C. Wylie, interview with author, 20 Jul 1987, NHC (hereafter Wylie Interview).

21. Ibid.; Hattendorf et al, *Sailors and Scholars,* p. 202.

22. J. C. Wylie, "On Maritime Strategy," *Proceedings* 79 (May 1953): 468.

23. Wylie Interview, 20 Jul 1987. "On Maritime Strategy" was, in fact, the most clearly stated pronouncement on naval strategy to appear in the postwar period. Others, notably Ernest M. Eller, had made the same point. See Eller, "Sea Power and Peace," *Proceedings* 73 (Oct 1947): 1165; and his 1950 prize essay entry "Will We Need a Navy to Win?" *Proceedings* 76 (Mar 1950): 245. Like Wylie, Eller thought the Navy should educate the American people on the uses of sea power. Ibid., p. 242. As a private individual, Huntington was free to speculate in an intelligent, informed manner and to write a more detailed treatise on the Navy's thinking.

24. Hattendorf et al., *Sailors and Scholars,* p. 204.

25. J. C. Wylie, "Why a Sailor Thinks Like a Sailor," *Proceedings* 83 (Aug 1957): 814. Wylie's publication, *Military Strategy* (New Brunswick, NJ, 1967), also distinguished him as "the Navy's leading public strategist of the 1950s and 60s." See Peter M. Swartz, *Addendum to "Contemporary U.S. Naval Strategy: A Bibliography"* (Annapolis, 1987), p. 53. Swartz terms Wylie's views "remarkably similar to the views expressed in the Maritime Strategy a generation later."

26. Burke Oral History, 2: 213.

27. The Navy's basic strategic concept, and Burke's understanding of it, is apparent in the study of attack carrier force levels completed in the fall of 1953 by the Strategic Plans Division. See Burke to list, 13 Oct

1953, A4, box 280, Strategic Plans. The study exceeded the mere argument for carrier force levels. It considered the world situation, especially in critical geographical areas; the Soviet threat; the United States' concept of war; Navy missions, objectives, and tasks; and a naval role in war.

28. See Eisenhower's message to Congress transmitting Reorganization Plan 6 of 1953 concerning the Department of Defense, 30 April 1953, in U.S. President, *Public Papers of the Presidents: Dwight D. Eisenhower: 1953* (Washington, 1960), 8: 225–38; U.S. Congress, *United States Statutes at Large,* 67: 638–39; and Joint Chiefs of Staff, *Joint Chiefs of Staff Special Historical Study: Chronology Functions and Composition of the Joint Chiefs of Staff* (Washington, n.d.), p. 210.

29. Wylie Interview, 20 Jul 1987.

30. Since the end of the Second World War, the Navy had resisted Air Force efforts to make nuclear strategy the nation's strategy. The debate ended under Eisenhower and naval leaders had little choice but to go along. Radford, who had resisted the effort in 1948–1950 and who had expressed reservations about the "superficial" Eisenhower as president, now heartily embraced affordable atomic defense and his new commander in chief. Radford to Denfeld, 14 Apr 1950, box 56, Radford Papers. Radford adopted the New Look primarily because he agreed with Eisenhower that the United States could not afford "conventional forces at the same time as nuclear forces." Baldwin Oral History, 2: 454–55.

31. That the Navy was prepared to make the transition is a tribute to the leadership of Admirals Nimitz, Denfeld, Radford, Sherman, and Carney. David A. Rosenberg and Floyd D. Kennedy, Jr., *History of the Strategic Arms Competition, 1945–1972,* Supporting Study: *U.S. Aircraft Carriers in the Strategic Role, Part 1—Naval Strategy in a Period of Change* (Falls Church VA, 1975), pp. 151–80; David Alan Rosenberg, "The Origins of Overkill: Nuclear Weapons and American Strategy, 1945–1960," *International Security* 7 (Spring 1983): 29.

32. Steinhardt to OP-30, 23 Dec 1953, enclosing OEG comments on preliminary study of attack carrier force levels, A4, box 230, Strategic Plans.

33. Burke to list, 15 Jan 1960, enclosing the strategic concept for antisubmarine warfare, Chronological file, CNO, Command File.

34. Trost, "Looking Beyond the Maritime Strategy," p. 16.

Bibliography

Primary Sources

MANUSCRIPTS

The Operational Archives of the Naval Historical Center, located in Washington, D.C., holds a rich collection of material on the post-World War II United States Navy, much of which for the 1946–1955 period has been declassified. Only unclassified and declassified records were used for this study.

The two most valuable sources for this work were the Strategic Plans Division Records and the Records of the Immediate Office of the Chief of Naval Operations, the 00 (Double Zero) File. The Strategic Plans Division, OP-30 during this period, came under the authority of the Deputy Chief of Naval Operations for Operations (OP-03). The collection contains not only draft and finished plans, but also relevant correspondence concerning Navy policy and strategy. The 00 File contains copies of studies and plans, as well as the correspondence.

The files of the CNO Secretariat, Joint Staff (JCS File), contain JCS plans and drafts and pertinent internal Navy correspondence concerning the service's views on various JCS plans.

How the Navy's strategic plans were implemented at the operational level becomes apparent in the records of the subordinate offices, which can be found in the post-World War II Command, Plans, and Report files. These collections also contain relevant materials prepared at the highest joint and service levels.

Of importance to the Navy's strategic planning, and especially to the interservice rivalry of the period, are the records of the Deputy Chief of Naval Operations for Air (OP-05) and the Organizational Research and Policy Division (OP-23), which contain the records of that staff and its precursors—the Radford Committee, SCOROR, and UNICOM.

The papers of Admirals Arthur Radford, Forrest Sherman, and Louis Denfeld were of particular help, although the Sherman collection is disappointingly small.

Important manuscripts held by the Operational Archives include Marx Leva's unpublished "Secretary of Defense James V. Forrestal in Retrospect: The View Back, after Fifteen Years," and handwritten and typed drafts of Admiral Radford's memoirs, the first part of which has been edited and published by Stephen Jurika, Jr. (listed in the bibliography). A second volume is forthcoming. The Operational Archives also holds a complete copy of the Forrestal diaries, the original of which is held by the Princeton University Library.

The Operational Archives' Biographical files and postwar Press Releases proved important reference sources on officers and events. A resource not to be overlooked by the researcher is the collection of Department of Defense phone listings.

DIARIES, MEMOIRS, AND PAPERS

Bohlen, Charles E. *Witness to History, 1929–1967.* New York: Norton, 1973.

Bradley, Omar N., and Clay Blair, Jr. *A General's Life.* New York: Simon and Schuster, 1983.

Bryant, Arthur. *Triumph in the West: A History of the War Years Based on the Diaries of Field-Marshal Lord Alanbrooke, Chief of the Imperial General Staff.* Garden City, NY: Doubleday, 1959.

Chandler, Alfred D., Jr., and Louis Galambos, eds. *The Papers of Dwight David Eisenhower.* 11 vols. Baltimore and London: Johns Hopkins University Press, 1970–1984.

Clark, J. J., and Clark G. Reynolds. *Carrier Admiral.* New York: David McKay Company, Inc., 1967.

Etzold, Thomas H., and John Lewis Gaddis, eds. *Containment: Documents on American Policy and Strategy, 1945–1950.* New York: Columbia University Press, 1978.

Jurika, Stephen, ed. *From Pearl Harbor to Vietnam: The Memoirs of Admiral Arthur W. Radford.* Stanford, CA: Hoover Institution Press, 1980.

Loewenheim, Francis L., Harold D. Langley, and Manfred Jonas, eds. *Roosevelt and Churchill: Their Secret Wartime Correspondence.* New York: E. P. Dutton & Co., Inc., 1975.

Millis, Walter, ed., with the collaboration of E. F. Duffield. *The Forrestal Diaries.* New York: Viking Press, 1951.

INTERVIEWS AND ORAL HISTORIES

Interviews with author. Naval Historical Center. Washington, DC.
Anderson, Herbert H., 22 July 1987.

Burke, Arleigh A., 9 July 1987.
Carney, Robert B., 2 July 1987.
Nunn, Ira H., 8 July 1987.
Wylie, J. C., 20 July 1987.
U.S. Naval Institute Oral History Collection. Annapolis, MD.
Baldwin, Hanson W. Interview with John T. Mason, Jr. 2 vols. 1976.
Bieri, Bernhard H. Interview with John T. Mason, Jr. 1970.
Burke, Arleigh A. Interview with John T. Mason, Jr. Special Series. 4 vols. 1979.
Dyer, George. Interview with John T. Mason, Jr. 1973.
Griffin, Charles D. Interview with John T. Mason, Jr. 2 vols. 1973.
Jurika, Stephen, Jr. Interview with John T. Mason, Jr. 2 vols. 1979.
Libby, Ruthven E. Interview with Paul Stillwell. 1984.
Columbia University Oral History Project. New York, NY.
Conolly, Richard. Interview with Donald F. Shaughnessy. 1960.
Fechteler, William M. Interview with John T. Mason, Jr. 1962.

CONGRESSIONAL AND EXECUTIVE DOCUMENTS

U.S. Congress. House. Committee on Armed Services. *Sundry Legislation Affecting the Naval and Military Establishments.* 81st Cong., 2d sess., 1950.
———. Committee on Armed Services. *Hearings on Military Posture and H.R. 1872 [S. 4040], Department of Defense Authorization for Appropriations for Fiscal Year 1980 and H.R. 2575 [S. 4291], Department of Defense Supplemental Authorization for Appropriations for Fiscal Year 1979 before the Seapower and Strategic and Critical Materials Subcommittee.* 96th Cong., 1st sess., 1979. Part 4.
———. Committee on Naval Affairs. *Sundry Legislation Affecting the Naval Establishment, 1945: Hearing on House Concurrent Resolution 80, Composition of the Postwar Navy.* 79th Cong., 1st sess., 1945, Item 110.
———. Subcommittee of the Committee on Appropriations. *Department of the Navy.* 81st Cong., 2d sess., 1950. Part 4.
———. Seapower and Strategic and Critical Materials Subcommittee of the Committee on Armed Services. *The 600-Ship Navy and the Maritime Strategy.* 99th Cong., 1st sess., 1985.
U.S. Congress. Senate. Subcommittee of the Committee on Appropriations. *Department of Defense Appropriations, 1951.* 81st Cong., 2d sess., 1950.
———. Subcommittee of the Committee on Appropriations. *Department of Defense Appropriations for 1953.* 82d Cong., 2d sess., 1952.
———. U.S. Department of the Navy. *Manual for the Office of the Chief of Naval Operations.* Washington: GPO, November 1945.
———. *Organizational Manual for the Office of the Chief of Naval Operations.* Washington: GPO, August 1948.

————. *Organizational Manual for the Office of the Chief of Naval Operations.* Washington: GPO, November 1950.

U.S. Department of State. *Foreign Relations of the United States: The Conferences at Washington and Quebec, 1943.* William Slany and Richardson Dougall, eds. Washington: GPO, 1970.

————. *Foreign Relations of the United States, 1950.* Vol. 1, *National Security Affairs: Foreign Economic Policy.* S. Everett Gleason and Frederick Aandahl, eds. Washington: GPO, 1977.

U.S. President. *Public Papers of the Presidents of the United States: Harry S. Truman.* 8 vols. Washington: GPO, 1961–1966.

————. *Public Papers of the Presidents of the United States: Dwight D. Eisenhower: 1953.* 8 vols. Washington: GPO, 1960–1961.

Secondary Sources

BOOKS

Albion, Robert Greenhalgh. *Makers of Naval Policy, 1798–1947.* Rowena Reed, ed. Annapolis, MD: Naval Institute Press, 1980.

Barker, Elisabeth. *The British Between the Superpowers, 1945–1950.* Toronto, Canada, and Buffalo, NY: University of Toronto Press, 1983.

Baylis, John. *Anglo-American Defense Relations, 1939–1984: The Special Relationship.* 2d. ed. New York: St. Martin's Press, 1984.

Bennett, Edward M. *Franklin D. Roosevelt and the Search for Security: American-Soviet Relations, 1933–1939.* Wilmington, DE: Scholarly Resources, Inc., 1985.

Best, Richard A., Jr. *"Cooperation with Like-Minded Peoples": British Influence on American Security Policy, 1945–1949.* New York, Westport, CT, and London: Greenwood Press, 1986.

Blair, Clay Jr. *Silent Victory: The U.S. Submarine War against Japan.* Philadelphia and New York: J. B. Lippincott, 1975.

Borowski, Harry R. *A Hollow Threat: Strategic Air Power and Containment before Korea.* Westport, CT, and London: Greenwood, 1982.

Borowski, Harry R., ed. *Military Planning in the Twentieth Century: Proceedings of the Eleventh Military History Symposium.* Washington: GPO, 1986.

Coletta, Paolo E. *The United States Navy and Defense Unification, 1947–1953.* Newark: University of Delaware Press, 1981.

Condit, Kenneth W. *History of the Joint Chiefs of Staff: The Joint Chiefs of Staff and National Policy.* Vol. 2, *1947–1949.* Washington: Joint Chiefs of Staff, 1978.

Davis, Lynn Etheridge. *The Cold War Begins: Soviet-American Conflict over Eastern Europe.* Princeton: Princeton University Press, 1974.

Davis, Vincent. *The Admirals Lobby.* Chapel Hill: University of North Carolina Press, 1967.

―――. *Postwar Defense Policy and the U.S. Navy, 1943–1946.* Chapel Hill: University of North Carolina Press, 1962.

De Santis, Hugh. *The Diplomacy of Silence: The American Foreign Service, the Soviet Union, and the Cold War.* Chicago and London: University of Chicago Press, 1981.

Dunn, Keith A., and William O. Staudenmaier, eds. *Military Strategy in Transition: Defense and Deterrence in the 1980s.* Boulder, CO, and London: Westview Press, 1984.

Friedman, Norman. *U.S. Aircraft Carriers: An Illustrated Design History.* Annapolis, MD: Naval Institute Press, 1983.

―――. *U.S. Destroyers.* Annapolis, MD: Naval Institute Press, 1982.

Futrell, Robert Frank. *Ideas, Concepts, Doctrine: A History of Basic Thinking in the United States Air Force, 1907–1964.* Maxwell Air Force Base: Air University, 1971.

Gaddis, John Lewis. *The Long Peace: Inquiries into the History of the Cold War.* New York and Oxford: Oxford University Press, 1987.

Gallicchio, Marc S. *The Cold War Begins in Asia: American East Asian Policy and the Fall of the Japanese Empire.* New York: Columbia University Press, 1988.

Gowing, Margaret, and Lorna Arnold. *Independence and Deterrence: Britain and Atomic Energy, 1945–1952.* Vol. 1, *Policy Making.* London: The Macmillan Press, Ltd., 1974.

Hamilton, Nigel. *Monty: Final Years of the Field-Marshal, 1944–1976.* New York: McGraw Hill, 1986.

Hammond, Paul Y. *Organizing for Defense: The American Military Establishment in the Twentieth Century.* Princeton: Princeton University Press, 1961.

Harbutt, Fraser J. *The Iron Curtain: Churchill, America, and the Origins of the Cold War.* New York and Oxford: Oxford University Press, 1986.

Hattendorf, John B., B. Mitchell Simpson III, and John R. Wadleigh. *Sailors and Scholars: The Centennial History of the U.S. Naval War College.* Newport, RI: Naval War College Press, 1984.

Hewlett, Richard G., and Francis Duncan. *Nuclear Navy, 1946–1962.* Chicago and London: University of Chicago Press, 1974.

Howard, Michael. *The Mediterranean Strategy in the Second World War.* New York and Washington: Frederick A. Praeger, Publishers, 1968.

Hurley, Alfred F., and Robert C. Ehrhart. *Air Power and Warfare.* Washington: Office of Air Force History, 1979.

International Institute for Strategic Studies. *The Military Balance, 1986–1987.* London: IISS, 1986.

Ismay, Lord. *NATO: The First Five Years, 1949–1954.* 2d ed. Utrecht, Netherlands: Bosch, 1956.

Joint Chiefs of Staff. *Joint Chiefs of Staff Special Historical Study: Chronology*

Functions and Composition of the Joint Chiefs of Staff. Washington: Joint Chiefs of Staff, n.d.

Komer, Robert W. *Maritime Strategy or Coalition Defense?* Cambridge, MA: Abt Books, 1984.

Kuniholm, Bruce Robellet. *The Origins of the Cold War in the Near East: Great Power Conflict and Diplomacy in Iran, Turkey, and Greece.* Princeton: Princeton University Press, 1980.

Love, Robert William Jr., ed. *The Chiefs of Naval Operations.* Annapolis, MD: Naval Institute Press, 1980.

NATO Information Service. *NATO Facts and Figures.* Brussels, Belgium: NATO Information Service, 1971.

Pogue, Forrest C. *George C. Marshall: Statesman, 1945–1949.* New York: Viking Press, 1987.

Polmar, Norman and Thomas B. Allen. *Rickover.* New York: Simon and Schuster, 1982.

Potter, E. B. *Nimitz.* Annapolis, MD: Naval Institute Press, 1976.

Rearden, Steven L. *History of the Office of the Secretary of Defense.* Vol. 1, *The Formative Years, 1947–1950.* Washington: Historical Office, Office of the Secretary of Defense, 1984.

Reynolds, Clark G. *The Fast Carriers: The Forging of an Air Navy.* Huntington, NY: Robert E. Krieger Publishing Company, 1978.

Rosenberg, David A. *Historical Perspectives in Long-Range Planning in the Navy.* Washington: Office of the Assistant Secretary of the Navy, 1980.

Rosenberg, David A., and Floyd D. Kennedy, Jr. *History of the Strategic Arms Competition, 1945–1972.* Supporting Study: US Aircraft Carriers in the Strategic Role, Part 1—Naval Strategy in a Period of Change: Interservice Rivalry, Strategic Interaction, and the Development of a Nuclear Attack Capability 1945–1951. Falls Church, VA: Lulejian and Associates, 1975.

Sherry, Michael S. *Preparing for the Next War: American Plans for Postwar Defense, 1941–1945.* New Haven, CT, and London: Yale University Press, 1977.

Schnabel, James F. *History of the Joint Chiefs of Staff: The Joint Chiefs of Staff and National Policy.* Vol. 1, *1945–1947.* Washington: Joint Chiefs of Staff, 1979.

Sherwood, Robert E. *Roosevelt and Hopkins: An Intimate History.* New York: Harper & Row, 1948.

Sternhell, Charles M., and Alan M. Thorndike. *Antisubmarine Warfare in World War II.* Washington: Office of the Chief of Naval Operations, 1946.

Swartz, Peter M. *Addendum to "Contemporary U.S. Naval Strategy: A Bibliography."* Annapolis, MD: Naval Institute Press, 1987.

Tidman, Keith R. *The Operations Evaluation Group: A History of Naval*

Operations Analysis. Annapolis, MD: Naval Institute Press, 1984.

Vlahos, Michael. *Blue Sword: The Naval War College and the American Mission, 1919–1941*. Newport, RI: Naval War College Press, 1980.

Waddington, C. H. *O.R. in World War 2: Operational Research against the U-boat*. London: Elek Science, 1973.

Watson, Robert J. *History of the Joint Chiefs of Staff: The Joint Chiefs of Staff and National Policy*. Vol. 5, *1953–1954*. Washington: Joint Chiefs of Staff, 1986.

Wettern, Desmond. *The Decline of British Seapower*. London: Jane's, 1982.

Wolfers, Arnold. *Discord and Collaboration: Essays on International Politics*. Baltimore: Johns Hopkins University Press, 1962.

Wylie, J. C. *Military Strategy*. New Brunswick, NJ: Rutgers University Press, 1967.

Yergin, Daniel. *Shattered Peace: The Origins of the Cold War and the National Security State*. Boston: Houghton Mifflin Company, 1977.

ARTICLES

Anderson, M. S. "British Public Opinion and the Russian Campaign of 1812." *Slavonic and East European Review* 34 (June 1956): 408–25.

Baldwin, Hanson W. "Shall We Police the World?" *Sea Power* 4 (March 1944): 6–8.

Beatty, Jack. "In Harm's Way." *The Atlantic Monthly* 259 (May 1987): 37–53.

Brodie, Bernard. "New Tactics in Naval Warfare." *Foreign Affairs* 24 (January 1946): 210–23.

Brooks, Linton F. "Naval Power and National Security: The Case for the Maritime Strategy." *International Security* 11 (Fall 1986): 58–88.

Bundy, McGeorge. "The Test of Yalta." *Foreign Affairs* 27 (July 1949): 618–29.

Cope, Harley. "When Peace Comes." U.S. Naval Institute *Proceedings* 69 (February 1943): 165–68.

Dingman, Roger. "Strategic Planning and the Policy Process: American Plans for War in East Asia, 1945–1950." *Naval War College Review* 32 (November–December 1979): 4–21.

Downing, Wayne A. "US Army Operations Doctrine: A Challenge for the 1980s and Beyond." *Military Review* 51 (January 1981): 64–73.

Eller, Ernest M. "Sea Power and Peace." U.S. Naval Institute *Proceedings* 73 (October 1947): 1161–73.

———. "Will We Need a Navy to Win?" U.S. Naval Institute *Proceedings* 76 (March 1950): 237–47.

Forrestal, James. "Keep the Navy to Keep the Peace." *Sea Power* 5 (July 1945): 21–22.

Halsey, Ashley, Jr. "A Slide-Rule Formula for a Post-War Navy." U.S. Naval Institute *Proceedings* 70 (April 1944): 371–84.

Hattendorf, John B. "The Evolution of the Maritime Strategy: 1977 to 1987." *Naval War College Review* 41 (Summer 1988): 7–38.

Hayward, Thomas B. "The Future of U.S. Sea Power." U.S. Naval Institute *Proceedings* 105 (May 1979): 66–71.

Huntington, Samuel P. "National Policy and the Transoceanic Navy." U.S. Naval Institute *Proceedings* 80 (May 1954): 483–93.

Kennan, George F. "Containment Then and Now." *Foreign Affairs* 65 (Spring 1987): 883–90.

[Kennan, George F.] "The Sources of Soviet Conduct." *Foreign Affairs* 25 (July 1947): 572–82.

Leva, Marx. "Barring the Door to the Med." U.S. Naval Institute *Proceedings* 113 (August 1987): 83–88.

Maddux, Thomas R. "United States-Soviet Naval Relations in the 1930's: The Soviet Union's Efforts to Purchase Naval Vessels." *Naval War College Review* 29 (Fall 1976): 33–35.

Mearsheimer, John J. "A Strategic Misstep: The Maritime Strategy and Deterrence in Europe." *International Security* 11 (Fall 1986): 3–57.

Melissen, Jan, and Bert Zeeman. "Britain and western Europe, 1945–51: opportunities lost?" *International Affairs* 63 (Winter 1986/87): 81–95.

Mott, C. W. "Barring the Door to the Med." "Comment and Discussion" Section. U.S. Naval Institute *Proceedings* 113 (December 1987): 110.

Muir, Malcolm, Jr. "American Warship Construction for Stalin's Navy Prior to World War II: A Study in Paralysis of Policy." *Diplomatic History* 5 (Fall 1981): 337–51.

Possony, Stefan T. "The Vindication of Sea Power." U.S. Naval Institute *Proceedings* 71 (September 1945): 1033–43.

Rosenberg, David Alan. "The Origins of Overkill: Nuclear Weapons and American Strategy, 1945–1960." *International Security* 7 (Spring 1983): 3–71.

———. "The U.S. Navy and the Problem of Oil in a Future War: The Outline of a Strategic Dilemma, 1945–1950." *Naval War College Review* 29 (Summer 1976): 53–64.

Sherman, Forrest P. "Air Operations in Palestine." U.S. Naval Institute *Proceedings* 53 (July 1927): 787–92.

———. "Air Tactics and Strategy." U.S. Naval Institute *Proceedings* 52 (May 1926): 855–65.

———. "Air Warfare." U.S. Naval Institute *Proceedings* 52 (January 1926): 62–71.

———. "The British Occupation of Guantanamo Bay." U.S. Naval Institute *Proceedings* 57 (April 1931): 509–512.

————. "Historical Ships of the Navy—*Essex*." "Discussion" Section. U.S. Naval Institute *Proceedings* 60 (April 1934): 550–51.

————. Review of *Economy and Naval Security,* by Sir Herbert Richmond. U.S. Naval Institute *Proceedings* 58 (June 1932): 911–13.

Smith-Hutton, H. H. "Post-War Problems and the Navy." U.S. Naval Institute *Proceedings* 69 (June 1943): 785–93.

Swartz, Peter M. "Contemporary U.S. Naval Strategy: A Bibliography." U.S. Naval Institute *Proceedings* 112 (January 1986 Supplement): 41–47.

Trost, Carlisle, and A. H. Trost, "Looking Beyond the Maritime Strategy." U.S. Naval Institute *Proceedings* 113 (January 1987): 13–16.

Ullman, Harlan K. "The Pacific and US Naval Policy." *Naval Forces* 6 (June 1985): 36–45.

Watkins, James D. "The Maritime Strategy." U.S. Naval Institute *Proceedings* 112 (January 1986 Supplement): 2–17.

Wylie, J. C. "On Maritime Strategy." U.S. Naval Institute *Proceedings* 79 (May 1953): 467–77.

————. "Why a Sailor Thinks Like a Sailor." U.S. Naval Institute *Proceedings* 83 (August 1957): 811–17.

NEWSPAPERS AND MAGAZINES

New York Times, September 1942.
Time, March 1950.

DISSERTATIONS AND THESES

Sokolsky, Joel J. "Seapower in the Nuclear Age: NATO as a Maritime Alliance." Ph.D. diss., Harvard University, 1986.

Index

ABOUT THE AUTHOR

Michael A. Palmer is a historian in the contemporary history branch of the Naval Historical Center in Washington, D.C. He holds a Ph.D. in military history from Temple University. His first book, *Stoddert's War: Naval Operations during the Quasi-War with France, 1798–1801,* published in 1987, won the Samuel Eliot Morison Award for Naval Literature and was named Book of the Year, for the best history of the era of the American Revolution, by the American Revolution Round Table of New York.

Dr. Palmer is also the author of numerous articles on a variety of subjects that have been published in some of this country's leading professional journals, including *Naval War College Review* and *Military Review.*

The **Naval Institute Press** is the book-publishing arm of the U.S. Naval Institute, a private, nonprofit professional society for members of the sea services and civilians who share an interest in naval and maritime affairs. Established in 1873 at the U.S. Naval Academy in Annapolis, Maryland, where its offices remain today, the Naval Institute has more than 100,000 members worldwide.

Members of the Naval Institute receive the influential monthly magazine *Proceedings* and discounts on fine nautical prints, ship and aircraft photos, and subscriptions to the quarterly *Naval History* magazine. They also have access to the transcripts of the Institute's Oral History Program and get discounted admission to any of the Institute-sponsored seminars regularly offered around the country.

The Naval Institute's book-publishing program, begun in 1898 with basic guides to naval practices, has broadened its scope in recent years to include books of more general interest. Now the Naval Institute Press publishes more than forty new titles each year, ranging from how-to books on boating and navigation to battle histories, biographies, ship and aircraft guides, and novels. Institute members receive discounts on the Press's more than 375 books.

Full-time students are eligible for special half-price membership rates. Life memberships are also available.

For a free catalog describing the Naval Institute Press books currently available, and for further information about U.S. Naval Institute membership, please write to:

Membership & Communications Department
U.S. Naval Institute
Annapolis, Maryland 21402
Or call, toll-free, (800) 233–USNI. In Maryland, call (301) 224–3378.

THE NAVAL INSTITUTE PRESS

ORIGINS OF THE MARITIME STRATEGY
THE DEVELOPMENT OF AMERICAN NAVAL STRATEGY, 1945–1955

Designed by Pamela L. Schnitter

Set in Schneidler by G & S Typesetters, Inc., Austin, Texas

Printed on 55-lb. Hi-Brite Vellum,
bound in James River Bamberger-Kaliko
with 80-lb., Multicolor Textured endsheets,
and stamped in APRL gold & #21 semi-matte
by Maple-Vail, Inc., York, Pennsylvania